COUNSELLING FOR TOADS

Toad, the famous character in Kenneth Grahame's *The Wind in the Willows*, is in a very depressed state and his good friends Rat, Mole and Badger are 'worried that he might do something silly'. . . .

> 'First they nursed him. Then they encouraged him. Then they told him to pull himself together. . . . Finally, Badger could stand it no longer. That admirable animal, though long on exhortation, was short on patience. "Now look here Toad, this can go on no longer," he said sternly. "There is only one thing left. You must have counselling!"'

Robert de Board's engaging account of Toad's experience of counselling will capture the imagination of the growing readership of people who are interested in counselling and the counselling process. In this sequel to the story of life on the River Bank, Toad and his friends come to life all over again. Heron, the counsellor, uses the language and the ideas of transactional analysis as his counselling method. Through the dialogues which make up the ten sessions or chapters of the book, Toad learns how to analyse his own feelings and develop his emotional intelligence. He meets his 'rebellious child' and his 'adult' along the way, and by the end of the book, as debonair as ever he was, is setting out on a completely new adventure. As readers learn about Toad, so they can learn about themselves and be encouraged to take the path of psychological growth and development.

Robert de Board, author of a best-selling textbook on counselling, says:

'Toad's experiences are based on my own work of counselling people over a period of twenty years. *Counselling for Toads* is really an amalgamation of the many counselling sessions I have held and contains a distillation of the truths I have learned from practice.'

Appropriate for anyone approaching counselling, whether as a student, client or counsellor, *Counselling for Toads* will appeal to both children and adults of all ages.

Robert de Board is an organisational consultant based in Henley-on-Thames. He is the author of two best-selling textbooks – *Counselling Skills* and *The Psychoanalysis of Organizations*.

COUNSELLING FOR TOADS

A Psychological Adventure

ROBERT de BOARD

London and New York

First published 1998 by Routledge
11 New Fetter Lane, London EC4P 4EE

Simultaneously published in the USA and Canada by Routledge
29 West 35th Street, New York, NY 10001

Reprinted 1998 (twice)

Grateful acknowledgement is made to the University Chest, Oxford,
for permission to use material from *The Wind in the Willows* by
Kenneth Grahame

Typeset in Palatino by Keystroke, Jacaranda Lodge, Wolverhampton
Printed and bound in Great Britain by Clays Ltd, St Ives PLC

British Library Cataloguing in Publication Data
A catalogue record for this book is available from the British Library

Library of Congress Cataloguing in Publication Data
A catalogue record for this book has been requested

ISBN 0–415–17429–5

Contents

Mole finds Toad in a poorly state

The weather was changing on the river bank. There was something ominous in the air that had not been there before. Black thunder-clouds hung menacingly over the fields. A few birds flitted pointlessly among the hedgerows singing a song, the notes of which they seemed scarcely able to remember. Even the ducks, who had as usual been quarrelling and quacking about supposed snubs and alleged insults, nestled into the reeds and chose to ignore all but the most outrageous attacks. Only the river moved on, black and sinuous, always changing yet always the same, creating a boundary for some animals, a highway for others, and with a suppressed energy and power that was only dangerous when ignored.

In this oppressive weather, Mole decided to go out. If he were to be honest, he was getting a bit restless, if not fed up, living with Rat. Yet even as he thought this, he felt guilty. For had not Ratty befriended Mole, taken him from his dull old house and introduced him to all his jolly friends? And what friends they were too; and what adventures they had had! Boating on the river, meeting Badger, caravanning with Toad and finally playing an heroic part in the rescue of Toad Hall from the Wild-wooders.

And yet, and yet. . . . Mole found it hard to describe exactly how he was feeling but it was something to do with his very self. In fact, that was it. He felt that he was rarely able to *be* himself because he was always standing in Rat's shadow. If they went boating, Rat would usually tell him that he was not doing it right, like not feathering his oars properly. When they moored, Rat would check the painter to see that Mole had secured it properly and invariably give it another turn around the post.

If they got lost, Rat always knew the way, just as he had done when he rescued Mole in a snowstorm in the Wild Wood. Or that time when, on a long walk, they chanced upon Mole's old house and, not unnaturally, Mole was overcome with emotion. Not so the ever-capable Rat, who took over, got the field mice to buy food and drink and organised a splendid evening.

The trouble was that the Rat *did* seem to be more capable than he was. He could scull better, he knew more knots and bends (he could even do a square lashing) and he really did take care of Mole. But in spite of this friendship and kindness, Mole felt dissatisfied. He wished that Rat wasn't *quite* so capable and that he would let Mole try out things in his own way, even if that meant getting it wrong. Of course, this had happened, like the first time he was in Rat's boat and grabbed the oars – and inevitably tipped the boat over. Rat had rescued him with great good humour and yet Mole thought, 'If I hear Rat tell that story at dinner ever again, I shall scream!'

Mole was thinking these thoughts as he put on his raincoat and sou'wester. He said to the Rat, 'I think I'll just pop over for a chat with Toad. We haven't seen him for ages and the walk will do me good.' The Rat, who was murmuring poetry things to himself and was trying to find a rhyme for 'effervescent', scarcely looked up but as Mole was going out of the door suddenly shouted, 'Be careful, Moley. Think of what happened last time you went out on your own!' He was of course referring to the time when Mole got lost in the Wild Wood and Rat had saved him. Mole was furious and called Rat several unflattering words under his breath. Out loud he said, 'Thank you Ratty. I'll take care,' adding *sotto voce*, 'you stupid, squint-eyed rodent', which Rat did not hear and which he was not meant to. But it made Mole feel better.

It was in this frame of mind that Mole walked over to Toad Hall, scarcely responding to the polite greetings of the rabbits he met on the way. He knew that he had gained their respect since arriving at the river bank and no one would demand any toll from him, as they once had done. Let them dare! And yet, did he only imagine that he heard one say in a rather horrid way, 'That's strange. You don't often see Mole on his own'?

In this rather miserable frame of mind, he found himself walking up the drive to Toad Hall. Toad Hall was impressive, there were no two ways about it. It had recently been described in a glossy county magazine as 'A gentleman's residence, benefiting from a secluded position on the bank of the river, enjoying expansive views across the Wild Wood and beyond. All this is surrounded by extensive and mature gardens with outlying paddocks and other buildings.' No wonder Toad was so proud of it.

But as Mole walked up the long drive, he was shocked to see how everything seemed run down. The hedges were untrimmed and the rose-beds were full of weeds.

The lawns were covered in leaves and the whole place looked unkempt and uncared for. Even the Hall itself looked grim and forbidding. The white paint, which used to sparkle in the sun, was dull and flaking. The creepers and climbing roses, which brought such colour and vibrancy to the walls, were dying and hanging down like black ropes. The windows, always clear and shiny, seemed only to reflect the dark and brooding weather and added to the atmosphere of grim foreboding. Mole shivered.

Pressing the buzzer he heard the bell ringing deep within the house. There was no answer and so he pressed a second time. Again the bell rang loudly, but to no avail. 'Oh well' thought Mole, 'I might have guessed that Toad would be out enjoying himself. He's probably at his club playing billiards.' This was a game at which Toad was particularly adept. Reluctant to leave, Mole walked around the house past the walled kitchen garden and came to the back door. He looked through the kitchen window to see what might be there. The room was empty, although there was some evidence that the stove was alight. He knew this room well, for it was furnished with comfortable old chairs in which he and Toad had sat and enjoyed many a hot mug of coffee on a winter's day. And then he saw, on a chair, a large heap of old clothes. Suddenly, the clothes started to move! Mole, being a timid creature, was about to run off into the garden when the clothes fell away to reveal . . . Toad! Mole tugged at the back door and was surprised to find that it opened. Inside was the saddest Toad he had ever seen. Toad's eyes, always large, were now hooded and dull. His cricket sweater, which he invariably wore around the house, was covered in food stains. And his plus-fours, usually immaculate and worn at just the right length, had the appearance of a couple of potato sacks hanging from his waist.

'Hello', said Toad. 'Sorry about the mess, but I'm not feeling too bright at the moment.' And with that, he burst into tears.

2

With friends like these . . .

As Mole walked back from Toad Hall later that day, his mind was in turmoil. How could Toad, that exciting and excitable animal, have got himself into such a sorry state?

Mole recalled the many hours he had spent with Toad over the years. No matter what he was doing, Toad was always smartly dressed to the point of parody. Mole especially remembered Toad's obsession with large motorcars and how he always dressed the part: large check overcoat and cape, an over-all linen dust-coat, a matching cap worn back-to-front, and goggles. And all of this complemented with a huge pair of yellow leather gauntlets.

At the time, Badger had pooh-poohed Toad's appearance, saying that he looked a guy and that no respectable animal would be seen dead with him But Badger was wrong. Mole thought he looked extremely dashing and compared his own rather sombre black smoking-jacket, which he habitually wore, to Toad's gay apparel.

Mole realised that Toad's ill-kempt appearance represented a serious internal change in his spirits. His previous smart and sometimes dramatic wardrobe represented and demonstrated the *élan* and *joie de vivre* of that singular animal. The bounce and swagger were perfectly displayed by loud tweed jackets, ample plus-fours and the whole set off with a pink Leander Club bow-tie. So what did it signify about Toad's emotional state that he was unwashed and ungroomed and wearing a sweater stiff with food droppings? And if Mole dared admit it, Toad, who always used a good cologne, was a bit smelly.

Later that night after their supper, Rat and Mole were sitting in front of a glowing fire, toasting their toes and sipping mugs of hot toddy. Mole had, of course, told Rat all about Toad and how he had found him. Since then the two friends had talked of nothing else. There was much 'tut-tutting' and 'What can we do?' and 'What can have caused it?' Gradually their conversation petered out as each animal sat staring into the fire, thinking his own thoughts.

Eventually Rat picked up the local weekly paper and thumbed through it in a desultory sort of way. Mole was half asleep when, suddenly, Rat sat bolt upright.

'Mole, listen to this!' he said in a commanding manner.

'Oh Ratty, you're not going through the small ads again, are you?' said Mole sleepily. Rat loved to see what bargains there were to be had, although he rarely found one.

'Be quiet,' said Rat in an unusually stern tone. 'Listen.' Then he proceeded to read out the following advertisement from the *Bankside Bugle*.

'"A qualified counsellor is now able to receive new clients. Animals who have personal problems which are causing them unhappiness or distress may care to make an appointment. Telephone Heronry 576."'

'Well,' said the Mole, who had not been listening very attentively, 'so what?'

'You perverse and foolish animal,' said the Rat, not for the first time. 'Don't you see? This could help poor Toady!'

Mole was by now fully awake. 'Surely you are not saying that Toad is in distress, are you? It's probably just a stomach upset. You know how Toad likes his food. And drink.'

It must be admitted that Toad could sometimes 'overdo things', as he called it, and had been known to drink more than was good for him. Rat and Mole rarely had more than a dry sherry or a glass of beer and took a puritanical view of Toad's occasional bender.

'No,' said Rat. 'Although I don't claim to understand these things, being myself a simple and uncomplicated creature.' (Here Mole coughed and spluttered into his mug and said it had gone down the wrong way.)

'But', the Rat continued, 'I am very worried about Toad, and I propose that you and I visit him tomorrow. I am worried that he might do something silly.' Although the Rat did not explain exactly what he meant by these words, both animals exchanged anxious looks.

'What's more, I think we should show Toad this advertisement about counselling and make him go.'

'Do you think he would?' asked Mole. 'After all, he can be a very self-willed and stubborn animal with a mind of his own.'

'You're quite right,' agreed the Rat. 'But if he is in the state of mind that you say he is, he will be putty in our hands!' With that, both animals retired to their beds, full of apprehension about the morrow and wondering how Toad would respond to their plan of help. For help him they would, whether he liked it or not.

And so it was that on the next morning, after breakfast, Mole found himself once again hurrying along the path to Toad Hall, this time accompanied by the Rat. As they walked, they discussed yet again Toad's unhappy situation and what might have caused it and how they would help him. Rat carried the newspaper which contained the announcement about counselling, although Mole had already memorised the telephone number. Suddenly, a deep voice somewhere to their left boomed out, 'Ratty, my dear little man. And Moley. What are you two doing here?'

Mole almost jumped out of his skin, but Rat said, 'It's only Badger' and as they peered into the wood on their left, the striped head and then the rest of Badger appeared.

'Well Badger,' said the Rat, 'what a surprise! I thought you would be at home slee—' He stopped in mid-sentence. 'I mean, working.'

'So I was,' said Badger, 'but I have some work to do here. In fact, it concerns a planning application and as I am a member of the District Council,' (Badger spoke these words in capital letters) 'I thought I would walk over and examine the matter personally.' He then said in his kindly way, 'But what are you doing here? You are both looking very serious.'

There was a clearing in the woods and the three animals sat down and Mole, helped by Rat, told Badger the sorry tale of Toad and the state in which Mole had found him and how, even at this minute, they were on their way to help that unhappy animal. Badger looked grim.

'I am not in the least surprised,' he said. 'It does not behove one to criticise one's friends, but (Mole had been waiting for this 'but') I have seen this coming for a long time. Toad, although he has many excellent qualities which I need not elaborate here, is essentially a weak and unstable animal. Bereft of his friends, who in the past have given him such good advice and told him precisely what he should do, he has let himself go and given way to silly and morbid thoughts. I shall therefore accompany you on your errand of mercy. He must be told, in no uncertain manner, to pull himself together!'

Mole and Rat were heartened by Badger's positive manner and determination and together the three comrades, arm-in-arm with Badger in the middle, walked purposefully towards Toad Hall. Fortunate Toad! Help was on the way.

3

Toad's first meeting with his counsellor

It would take too long to narrate all that happened over the next few days. First Toad was nursed by his friends. Then they encouraged him. Then they told him, quite sternly, to pull himself together. Finally, they spelled out the drab and dismal future facing him unless he 'got a grip of himself', as Badger eloquently put it.

But none of this had any effect on Toad. He responded as best he could, but there were no signs of the old Toad, full of life and eager to outwit their well-meant exhortations. Instead he remained sad and depressed, and the more his friends advised him in detail what he should do, the more sad and depressed he became.

Finally, Badger could stand it no longer. That admirable animal, though long on exhortation, was short on patience.

'Now, look here Toad, this can go on no longer. We are all trying to help you, but it seems you won't (or can't, thought Mole perceptively) help yourself. There is only one thing left. You must have counselling!'

There was a shocked silence. Even Toad sat up a little straighter. None of the animals knew fully what counselling meant, but they knew it was a mysterious activity undertaken by people who had experienced some severe or shocking event. The Rat, who was a traditionalist at heart, said, 'Do you really think Toad is that bad? I mean, don't you think it's a bit trendy, all this counselling? It seems from the newspapers that everyone these days is given counselling. In my day, people in trouble were given a couple of aspirin. It probably did them more good.' Ratty remembered that the original suggestion about counselling had come from him and he was beginning to get cold feet.

'But we've got the address of a local counsellor,' said the Mole. 'I thought we had agreed that Toad ought to see him. I agree with Badger.'

'Well said, Mole,' answered Badger. 'You mustn't be worried, Ratty. Toad must be in a very poor state of health if even the advice *I* can offer appears to fall on deaf ears. I know that you can be obstinate, Toad, but it does seem that you need some kind of help which, surprisingly, your friends cannot give you. Desperate circumstances require desperate remedies. We must try counselling.'

And so it happened that, after much telephoning and arranging and pushing and pleading, Toad arrived at a large house called The Heronry. It was a foursquare, three-storeyed building of red brick mellowed to a terra-cotta colour with occasional bands of yellow. It had an air of permanence and sensible values and looked the sort of house where a family might remain for a long time. After ringing the bell, Toad was shown to a book-lined room with some chairs and a large desk on which sat odds and ends, including a china head with words written all over the skull. It bore the legend 'Phrenology by L. N. Fowler'.

The Heron entered, looking tall and wise, and sat on the chair opposite Toad. He wished Toad good morning and then sat quietly looking at him. Toad, who had become used to people talking at him, waited for the lecture to begin. But nothing happened. In this silence, Toad could feel the blood pulsing in his head and it seemed as if this was pumping up the tension in the room. He began to feel very uncomfortable. The Heron continued to look at him. Finally Toad could stand it no longer.

'Aren't you going to tell me what to do?' he asked plaintively.

'About what?' answered Heron.

'Well, tell me what I have to do to get better.'

'Are you feeling unwell?'

'Yes, I am. But surely they have told you all about me?'

'Who are "they"?' asked Heron.

'Oh, you know. Badger and Rat and all that lot.' And with those words, Toad started to cry and let loose a flood of unhappiness that, all unknowingly, he had kept pent up for a long time. The Heron remained silent but pushed a box of paper tissues nearer to him. Eventually Toad's sobs subsided and he drew breath, and he felt a little better. Then the Heron spoke.

'Would you like to tell me why you are here?'

'I am here', said Toad, 'because they made me come. They said that I needed counselling and they got your name from the newspaper. And I am ready to listen to you and do whatever you think best. I know that they have my best interests at heart.'

The Counsellor shifted in his chair. 'So who is my client, you or them?'

Toad did not quite understand.

'Look,' said the Counsellor, 'your friends want me to counsel you so that their worry about you will be relieved. You seem to want to be helped in order to please

them. So I think that my client is really your friends.'
Toad was confused by all this and clearly showed it.

'Perhaps we can clarify the situation,' said the
Counsellor. 'Who is going to pay for these meetings?'

I might have guessed, thought Toad. He's just like the
rest of them, only anxious about getting paid.

'You don't need to worry about that,' said Toad, feeling
a little like his old self. 'Badger said he would take care
of the money side of things. You will get paid, never fear.'

'Thank you,' said the Counsellor, 'but I am afraid
that this won't do at all. I suggest that we conclude this
meeting and put it down to experience.'

For the first time in many days, Toad began to feel
angry. 'Look here,' he said in a stronger voice, 'you can't
do that. You call yourself a counsellor and I have come
here for counselling. I have sat here waiting for you to tell
me something and now all you can say is that my money
isn't good enough. What more do I have to do to get
things started?'

'That is a very good question and I will answer
it,' the Counsellor responded. 'Counselling is always a
voluntary process, both for the counsellor and for the
client. That means we can only work together if you want
to do this for your *own* sake and not just to please your
friends. If we agree to work together we need to make a
contract, and then, at the completion of our work, I would
send my invoice to you. You see, it's not a question of
money. But this can only be your responsibility and no
one else's.'

Toad's mind was racing. Without understanding the
full import of the words, he realised that somehow
he was being asked to take responsibility for his own
counselling. And yet *he* was not the counsellor!

At the same time, the Counsellor had used the word

14

'work' and this implied Toad's active involvement in whatever might happen. All this was a long way from his initial attitude of waiting for somebody to tell him what to do. These thoughts were disturbing but at the same time, exciting. Maybe there was a way out of his misery which he could discover for himself. After what seemed an age, Toad spoke.

'I seem to have made rather an ass of myself and not for the first time. But I think I am beginning to see what you are getting at and I would like to work with you. Can we start again?'

'I rather think that we have started already,' replied the Counsellor. He then went on to spell out in detail what it would mean if they agreed to work together on a counselling programme.

'We would meet together for an hour once a week, for as long as required. I suggest every Tuesday at ten in the morning, starting next week. At the final session we will review what we have done and what you have learnt and you can consider any future plans you may wish to make.'

'And how much do you charge?' asked the practical Toad.

'Forty pounds per session,' replied Heron. 'I will invoice you for that amount at the completion of each session.' Then after a considerable pause he added, 'Well, have you decided what you would like to do?'

Toad did not often make considered decisions. Either he made them on the spur of the moment and lived to regret it, like driving off in a motorcar which just happened to take his fancy, or else he did what he was told, usually by Badger, and felt miserable as a result. He would have liked to have asked the sensible Rat, 'Ratty, what do you think I should do?' and have the responsibility taken from his shoulders. But the Heron was looking at him in a particular way as if he was quite certain that he, Toad, would make a sensible decision. He finally said, 'I would like to work with you and try to discover why I am feeling so miserable and what I can do to improve things. I have got my diary here. Shall we agree on those dates?'

As the Counsellor was seeing Toad to the door, Toad turned to him and said, 'Do you think that there is some hope for me of getting better?'

The Heron stopped and looked him straight in the eye. 'Toad, if I did not think that we are all capable of change and improvement, I would not be doing this work. It is not inevitable that things get better. But what I can promise is that you will have my full and undivided attention. And I shall expect the same commitment from you. If we both work together like that then we can expect a positive outcome. However, in the last analysis, it all depends on you.'

Toad walked down the path, trying to understand what those words meant.

4

Why Toad feels so depressed

Toad found that the ensuing week went by very slowly. He felt listless and kept waking early and having sad and morbid thoughts. He usually felt better as the day wore on but in the evenings he found that he began to feel quite anxious. He made himself go for a walk every day and although there was some wintry sunshine, it seemed to him that he saw everything in monochrome, like an old sepia photograph.

Initially his friends visited him and tried to cheer him up. He and the Rat played many games of cribbage ('Fifteen two, fifteen four and a pair's six') and the Mole tried to amuse him with all the latest river-bank news ('You'll never believe what Otter got up to last week!'). Badger would sit watching the proceedings and then, when there was a silence, he would begin a long and not entirely uninteresting story concerning his adventures as a young animal with Toad's father ('And there we were miles from home and not a penny in our pockets, when I thought up this rather clever idea'). After all this, Toad would retire to bed exhausted, only to wake at three in the morning and toss and turn until dawn.

When Tuesday finally arrived, Toad experienced a variety of emotions as he walked slowly towards the Heronry. He felt some relief that, at last, the day was here when he would see the Counsellor again, although he had very mixed feelings towards him. He felt anxious about what might be said and what might be done. Already, he had had to fight quite hard to be allowed to make the journey on his own. But if he had learnt anything from the first encounter, it was that the work he had to do could only be done by himself. He was beginning to realise that he had better start to grow up.

For the second time he found himself sitting in the study, with the Counsellor opposite him. Again there was silence and Toad experienced the same mounting pressure and increasing anxiety. Eventually the Counsellor spoke.

'Well Toad, how are you feeling today?'

'Quite well, thank you,' replied Toad, in the words that he had been taught to say as a very little toad and which he now used automatically as the unthinking response to this question. It actually meant nothing. But the Counsellor was not interested in verbal trivia.

'Let me ask you again. How are you really feeling?'

Toad felt very uncomfortable. 'How do you mean exactly, "feeling"?'

Toad was not being deliberately obtuse. Like many people, he had never consciously considered his own emotions in such a way that he could describe them to himself, let alone to anyone else. In fact, he had developed many behavioural strategies, albeit unconsciously to avoid the possibility of gaining self-knowledge. He had become a great 'greeter' and his well-known opening gambit on meeting other animals was a hearty 'Hello, you fellows,' followed by something like, 'You'll never

18

guess what I've been doing!' or else, 'Come and see this.' Consequently, no one ever asked him how he was, let alone how he felt.

So it was a new and unsettling experience to be asked, 'How are you feeling?', especially by someone who seemed to be genuinely interested in his answer. But because Toad had never indulged in self-analysis, he genuinely did not know how to describe his internal state.

'Let me ask the question in a different way,' said the Counsellor. 'Suppose we had a sort of thermometer that could measure how you are feeling. It has a ten-point scale. The lowest point on the scale is one, which means that you are feeling awful and probably suicidal. The mid-point is five and means that you are not feeling too bad. Ten is the highest point and means that you are feeling euphoric.' There was a flip-chart next to the Counsellor on which he drew his 'Feelings Thermometer'. Then he handed Toad the crayon and said, 'Where would you say you are now, Toad?' Without hesitation, Toad put a mark on the scale, midway between one and two.

'Have you ever had suicidal thoughts?' asked the Counsellor in a straightforward sort of way. This was a shocking question to ask and it frightened Toad to hear it. And yet at the same time it came as something of a relief.

'Yes, I have,' he replied quietly. 'About three months ago, things seemed so black that I could see no way out and I thought that I might do something silly. But that was before Mole found me. Since then, I have still felt depressed, but I haven't had those awful thoughts. And', he continued with a little more spirit, 'I certainly would not do anything like that now.'

'So how do you feel now?' Again, that same question.

'I feel', said Toad, 'as if I don't have much value. I keep thinking that I have made a mess of my life. Not like Rat or Mole or especially Badger, who are well respected. I'm a bit of a joke really. Oh yes, kind-hearted they say and good for a laugh. And generous to a fault. "Good old Toady" they say. But what have I done with my life? What have I ever achieved?' And here Toad broke into sobs that racked his frame.

The Counsellor pushed the paper tissues towards him. After a while he asked, 'Have you always felt like this?'

'Yes, I suppose I have, on and off, for a long time. Mind, I do have times when things seems better and I can get really involved in something. But then my spirits start to fall and I seem to lose interest. It's then that I get into what I can only describe as my familiar sad feelings. And that is how I'm feeling now.'

'So what do you think made you feel unhappy this time?' the Counsellor asked.

'It's quite a long story,' said Toad.

'I'm listening,' said the Counsellor.

So Toad began.

'I am sure that you know all about my escape from prison and about washer-women and barges and horses and motorcars. These are not events in my life of which I am particularly proud. Nor do I wish to deny them. But they have been talked about a lot and published, so I mean to say no more about them. Unless you ask me.' Toad stopped and looked enquiringly at the Heron, who gave no response, so he continued.

'Of course, those events had an enormous effect on me, but I think I would have got over them, as in many ways I have done. What really hurt was the horrid way I was treated on my return.'

'Do you remember anything in particular?' asked Heron.

'Yes, I do. I can't stop going over those events in my mind, time and time again, until I can almost enumerate each incident.'

'What's the first of these?' asked Heron.

'Well,' Toad continued, 'to begin with, after my rather clever final escape when I was being chased by a crowd of hooligans and busybodies, by a piece of sheer bad luck I fell into the river and nearly drowned. Fortunately, Ratty pulled me out of the water and I shall never cease to be grateful to him.'

'I don't quite understand,' said Heron. 'Why should that make you feel unhappy?'

'Because of his attitude,' replied Toad. 'Naturally, I was dying to tell him all about my adventures and I began to recount them even before my clothes were dry. But instead of being interested, Rat accused me of "swaggering" and insisted that I go and change and try and look like a gentleman, "if I could". Just imagine! I hadn't seen him for months and that's how he spoke to me.'

'So how did that you make you feel?' asked Heron.

'Initially I felt angry. After all, I'd had enough of being ordered about in prison. But I was still feeling grateful to Rat for rescuing me so I did as he said. We had lunch (I was starving) and I told Rat all about my adventures. You know, they are really interesting and much more exciting than Rat's rather dull life.'

'So how did he respond?' asked Heron.

'You won't believe it but what he actually said was, "Don't you see what an awful ass you've been making of yourself?" That really hurt me. I felt as if I had been reprimanded.' And Toad's eyes filled with tears at this unhappy memory.

'What did you do then?' asked the Heron.

'I did what I always do, I suppose. I feel uncomfortable when people are displeased with me, so I try to placate them and deflect their anger. I would promise to do almost anything to make them like me again. So I admitted that I had been an awful ass and promised I would improve my behaviour.'

'Did it work?' asked the Heron.

'How do you mean "work"?' asked Toad.

'Did it stop Rat being displeased with you?'

'I'm not sure,' answered Toad. 'Because he then told me the awful news that Toad Hall had been captured by the Wildwooders. Now this made me really angry. I don't often get angry, but I was then. Without thinking, I rushed out to recapture my beloved home. But the Wildwooders were in control and I almost got a bullet in my brain. And then they sank my boat so that by the time I returned to Rat's place, I was wet and exhausted and feeling in very low spirits. And I had only been home half a day! It wasn't fair. It really wasn't fair.' And Toad started to sob again at these unhappy memories.

Heron sat quietly listening to all of this and watched Toad closely but said nothing. Toad's sobs gradually turned into sniffs and he looked the picture of misery, with some strands of snot hanging from his nose. Again, Heron passed him the box of tissues and, like a little child, Toad obediently took some and blew his nose and wiped his eyes. After a while, Heron said, 'So how did the Rat greet you this time?'

Toad struggled to keep his voice under control. 'How did Rat greet me? You won't believe it but he was angry with me again! He called me a "trying animal" and said that he did not know how I managed to keep any friends at all. I have to admit that I can understand him feeling a bit annoyed. After all, it was his boat that was sunk, but that wasn't my fault. And anyhow, he knew I would pay for a new one. As I have done,' he added in a rather whining tone.

'So how did you respond to that?' asked Heron.

'In the same sort of way, I suppose, trying to placate him. I remember grovelling and saying that I had been headstrong and wilful and that I promised to be humble and submissive in the future. When I think of that now, I cringe with embarrassment and wonder how I could ever have said it. But I would say anything to stop people being angry with me and telling me off. Especially Ratty, who I thought was my friend.'

'So did you start to feel better after this?' enquired the Heron.

'Well, I did for a minute,' answered Toad. 'I remember Mole came in then and he was about the only person who showed any interest in my adventures. But just as I started to tell him some of the really interesting bits, in came the one person who can really frighten me.'

'Who is that?' asked the Heron.

'Badger,' replied Toad.

'Why?'

Toad answered immediately. 'Well, for a start, he's big and strong and can seem quite threatening. And when he gives me that stern look, he reminds me of my father, who was always criticising me. Anyhow, Badger told me off, good and proper, just as I knew he would. I can still remember his exact words: "Toad, you bad, troublesome little animal, aren't you ashamed of your-self? What would your father have said about these goings on!" I was so upset by his disapproval that I burst into tears and couldn't say a thing.'

Here Toad paused, overcome by these unhappy

23

memories, and strove to hold back his imminent tears. After a while, he was able to continue. 'Badger then said that he would let bygones be bygones and we started to make plans to recapture Toad Hall that night. Badger was obviously the leader although it was my house we were going to rescue. I didn't mind that, because with all his faults, Badger does seem to be a natural leader. But he seemed to go out of his way to humiliate me.'

'How did he do that?' asked the Heron.

'He told us that there was a secret passage leading up to the Hall. I knew nothing about this, but Badger said that my father had told him of it. But the point was that he referred to Father as "a worthy animal, a lot worthier than some others I could mention", and he looked straight at me when he said this. It made me feel extremely uncomfortable.' Again Toad stopped and swallowed and sniffed and showed every sign of someone working bravely to withstand emotions which were too great to bear. Eventually he was able to continue.

'And as if that wasn't enough, he went on to say that Father had told him not to tell me because – and I can remember his exact words – "He's a good boy, but very light and volatile in character!" All the others looked at me and I put on a brave face and talked a lot of nonsense to cover my embarrassment, but inside I felt humiliated.' Toad paused and reflected on those unhappy feelings.

After a while, the Heron asked, 'Anything else?'

'Yes,' answered Toad. 'But I don't want to go on. It makes me too upset. Anyhow, you can see why I started to feel miserable. Everyone was being so horrid to me. And it wasn't my fault.'

There was a long silence, during which neither of them spoke. Then the Heron said, 'This seems a good place to stop and see if there is anything to be learnt from all this.'

'Do you mind if I walk around a bit?' asked Toad. 'My back's getting a bit achey.'

The Heron looked stern. 'I can't give you permission to make your own decisions, Toad. What do you want to do?'

'I want to walk around a bit,' said Toad with some spirit, and under his breath he added, 'And I bloody well will, too!'

'Now,' said Heron, 'as a result of listening to your story, I have one question to ask.'

'What's that?' asked Toad, resuming his seat.

'What state would you say you were in during these incidents?'

'I don't understand you,' said Toad. 'What do you mean by "state"?'

'I mean', replied the Heron, 'what words could you use to describe how you were feeling and acting during these events which you have just related?'

'Well, I've told you. I was feeling very unhappy and miserable and guilty and criticised.'

'So let me ask you again,' replied the Heron. 'What state were you in?'

Toad sat still and thought deeply. He was not given to concentrated thought but now he reviewed in his mind these unhappy events to see what general lesson he could learn from each particular incident.

'I suppose', he said slowly, 'that you could say that I was feeling like I used to feel when I was little. Was I feeling like a child? Is that what you mean?'

'It's more what *you* mean, Toad. Does it sound right to you?'

'Yes, it does. Yes, of course it does.' Toad sounded increasingly positive. 'That's just how I was feeling. It's how I felt when I was a child and I had been severely reprimanded by my father.'

'So let's call that the Child Ego State,' said the Heron.
Toad looked puzzled.

'It's really quite simple,' said the Heron. 'You will
remember from your schooldays that "ego" is the Latin
for "I". And if we ask "What sort of a state is he in?" we
are asking "What mode of existence is he in?" So when
I say that someone is in the Child Ego State, I mean that
they are behaving and feeling like a child. It doesn't mean
"childish", rather "childlike".'

'I think I understand,' said Toad. 'But is it a bad thing
to be in this Child State?'

'It's neither good nor bad,' answered the Heron. 'It
just describes how someone actually *is*. Perhaps a better
question to ask is "How effective is it to be in the Child
State?"'

'Well,' said Toad, 'I don't think your question is very
helpful because you obviously can't help getting in a
state. So whether it's effective or not is beside the point.
It obviously depends on the kind of person you are. And
that's something you have no control over.'

'Is that so?' asked the Heron. 'Are you in the Child
State now?'

'No, of course I'm not. I'm talking to you.'

'So why is that?'

'Oh, I don't know why,' said Toad peevishly. 'I wish
you would stop picking on me. It's not fair. My brain
hurts. You're asking me too many questions. I'm not a
psychologist, you know.'

'In that case,' said the Heron, 'we had better stop.' And
so they did.

5

The next meeting

Toad met the Counsellor the following week and sat in his usual seat. He was surprised how quickly he was getting used to the routine and he now thought of the chair as 'his' chair. Sometimes he wondered if anyone else ever sat in it, or if the room was only used once a week for him.

But the thing that impressed him most about these counselling sessions was receiving the Heron's full and undivided attention. Toad began to realise that he had never before received anyone's full attention in his entire life. Whether he had ever given it to anyone was a question yet to be asked.

The Heron listened to him attentively all the time. It was as if, for an hour, he centred himself entirely on Toad and focused on his situation to the exclusion of all else. Consequently, he found that he did not have to keep saying, 'Do you see what I mean?' or 'Have I made myself clear?', which he habitually found himself using to excuse his waffle and imprecision.

Providing that he, Toad, found the words to describe what he was thinking, the Heron listened and understood. But when he failed to understand, he would say so and then Toad would be forced to be more precise and search for other words and expressions which would convey his meaning more exactly.

Somehow, the way in which the Heron listened to him and prodded him with questions enabled him to bring all sorts of thoughts and feelings to consciousness. Gradually he was beginning to explore and examine aspects of himself of which previously he had been unaware. In other words, Toad had started to learn.

'Well, Toad,' said the Heron. 'How are you feeling?' This question no longer surprised him and in fact he was expecting it.

'I'm feeling different,' he answered. 'I'm still low in my spirits, but I keep finding myself thinking about our previous meeting, when you talked about the Child Ego State. Are we going to talk about it any more this time?'

'Yes,' said the Heron. 'I would like to explore that with you. But it means that I must change roles.'

'What do you mean?' asked Toad.

'It means', replied the Heron, 'that I shall behave differently. If I am to teach you about the Child State, I must take on the role of the teacher. One of the differences will be that I shall be in a telling mode, rather than a listening mode. If I successfully teach you about the Child Ego State, then you will be able to use those ideas to explore your own self and your own experience. Remember, there is nothing so practical as a good theory!'

As Toad was trying to puzzle out just what that meant, the Heron stood up and went to the flip-chart.

'The Child Ego State', he began, 'is made up of the archaic relics of our childhood. It consists of all the emotions we experienced when we were little. You must remember that at birth, we start out with only the very basic emotions. In our early years, these gradually develop into more subtle and complex patterns of behaviour which become central to our very self and form part of us, defining our behaviour for the rest of our lives. The result is that now, in particular situations and circumstances which are different for each of us, we respond automatically from that basic position. Once again, we act and feel like the child we once were.'

'Could you explain that a bit more, please?' asked Toad.

'Certainly,' replied the Heron. 'I am suggesting that we are born with certain basic emotions, rather like the primary colours, which are similar for all babies. But as we develop as individuals, our feelings and responses become increasingly individualistic, just as basic colours mix together to create all sorts of subtle shades and hues. Does that make sense?'

'Yes,' said Toad, 'I can understand that.'

'Right then,' answered the Heron. 'What do you think these basic emotions are?' Toad frowned and scratched his head, but was unable to come up with an answer.

'Look at it this way,' said the Heron. 'I know you are not married, but do you have any nephews or nieces?'

'Yes, of course,' said the Toad, 'I always remember their birthdays and I love taking them their presents at Christmas. In fact, I think they're rather fond of me.'

'Good,' replied the Heron. 'So how would you define some of their basic emotions?'

'Well, they are usually rushing about all over the place, having fun. I don't know where they get all that energy! And then when I arrive, all laden with presents, they throw themselves at me and give me the most tremendous kisses and hugs. Very cheering, really. Mind you,' continued Toad, 'it's not just the presents. I get the same kind of welcome whenever I go. They're just very affectionate.'

'I'm sure they are,' said Heron. 'Let's write this up.' So he went to the flip-chart and wrote the heading 'Children's Basic Emotions' and underneath, 'Fun and Affection'.

'Any others?' the Heron asked.

'They can certainly get angry with each other,' said Toad. 'I've known them have the most terrible fights when I have had to separate them physically. They can be little devils.'

'So there's another basic emotion,' said Heron, and wrote 'Anger' on the chart.

'Oh yes,' said the Toad, 'I certainly agree with that.'

'Can you think of any others?' asked Heron.

'I'm a bit stuck,' Toad replied, after a pause.

'Try thinking of it in another way,' said the Heron. 'What are the basic emotions we seem to be born with, which just come naturally, without having to be learnt?'

'I'm not sure if this is what you are after,' said Toad, 'but my little nephews and nieces can easily get upset and sad. I remember on my last visit, they were crying because their puppy had just died. I tried to comfort them, they were all in tears. But I wasn't much help. Ended up crying myself. I'm really very soft-hearted, you know.' Here Toad blew his nose and fiddled with his bow-tie and his eyes were bright with tears.

'That seems like a very basic emotion,' said the Heron and wrote 'Sadness' on the list. 'Any others?'

Toad shook his head. 'I can't think of one.'

'How about fear?' asked the Heron. 'In my experience, children can easily become scared and it's very easy to frighten a child. Unbelievably, some adults seem to enjoy doing just that, but that's another story. Anyhow, do you agree with fear?'

30

'Most certainly,' Toad replied. 'I can still remember waking up screaming from my first nightmare when I was very small. And no one taught me to behave like that. I just yelled. It came naturally.'

'Right,' said the Heron. 'So I think that completes our list,' and he added 'Fear' to it. So this was what was finally written on the flip-chart:

Children's Basic Emotions

Fun and Affection

Anger

Sadness

Fear

'All of these emotions added together make up what is called the "Natural Child" and this forms a significant part of the total Child Ego State,' said the Counsellor.

'So', said Toad, 'when I see someone being affectionate, or getting angry or sad or frightened, I can say that they are in their Natural Child. Is that right?'

'Exactly,' said the Heron, 'although anger is more complex and we shall learn more about that particular emotion later on.'

'And people can be in their Child State no matter how old they are?' asked Toad.

'Most certainly,' replied the Heron. 'People get into their Child State and feel and act exactly the same as they did when they were little, quite irrespective of their chronological age.'

There was a long silence as Toad fell into deep thought. Finally he spoke.

'I think', he said, 'that I am often in the Child Ego State,' and lapsed back into silence.

'But', said Heron, 'that's only half the picture.'

'What do you mean?' said Toad. 'Is there more to be said about this Child Ego State?'

'There certainly is,' replied Heron. 'A great deal more. As we have seen, a child's natural behaviour is a mixture of these basic emotions,' and he pointed to the list on the flip-chart.

'For instance, a baby will scream for food and attention, drink as much milk as it can get and then sleep when it is replete and content. All those natural feelings come into operation from day one and as the baby grows physically stronger so its emotional life develops and becomes more powerful.

'But there are other factors which come into play. And the most important of these is the baby's parents. They impinge on its consciousness right from the beginning. Almost everything the baby does causes some response from its mother or father and these have a profound influence on the child.

'Usually a mother responds to her baby's cry with love and comforting behaviour. But parents can act in an unloving way. The mother may be tired or even ill and respond harshly. Or the father may have strict views on how children should be reared and may deliberately ignore the baby's cries for fear of "spoiling" it.'

'It makes you realise just how vulnerable babies are,' Toad said thoughtfully. 'I never realised before just what power people have over their children. They have total dominion. They can love them or reject them, cuddle them or abuse them. It's just a lottery what sort of parents you get.'

He sat very quietly, thinking deeply about his own childhood, trying to remember what it felt like. After a while, the Heron spoke again.

'You're quite right, Toad,' he said. 'Most parents try

to do their best and very few want anything but good for their children. But parents are only human and they inevitably pass on their beliefs and behaviours to their offspring as surely as they pass on their genes. And children just have to learn to cope and defend themselves from the consequences.'

'But how can they learn to cope?' asked Toad, now quite animated and obviously thinking hard. 'Babies and little children can't think logically. They can't sit down and plan how to cope with their mother's or father's behaviour.' He said this quite strongly, as if he was dealing, not with an abstruse point of child psychology, but with something deeply personal. As indeed he was.

'Well, of course a baby or an infant can't think through these issues logically or consciously,' said Heron. 'But what they do is to learn through experience. This kind of learning involves not just our brains but our total self. What we learn is a strategy for living. We develop behaviours which enable us to cope with our parents and others. And if we are lucky, we have enough energy left over to enjoy life.

'This means that every baby must learn how to adapt his or her basic behaviour to cope with their primal situation. These adaptations become the nucleus around which the rest of our behaviour grows and develops. Of course, we are influenced by many other events later in our lives. But these earliest experiences shape the beginning of us and we can never deny or forget them.'

'Could you slow down a bit?' pleaded Toad. 'Just when I think that I have grasped something, you go on to something else.'

'I'm sorry,' smiled the Heron. 'I know that I tend to go on a bit about this, but I believe it to be of the greatest importance. In all our work together, Toad, understanding your childhood is the key to understanding yourself. As Freud said, "Where there is Id, there shall Ego be." But I'll explain that later. Now Toad, what was it in particular that you did not understand?'

'You said that as we learn to cope with our lives as infants, we have to make "adaptations" to our natural behaviour. What does that mean?'

'That's an excellent question,' answered Heron. 'Let me answer by telling you a short story. It's science fiction, so you can let your imagination run free.

'Imagine a small planet on which there are only three living beings, yourself and two others. These two other beings are more than twice your height and you are completely dependent on them for everything. This includes not only your food but also your emotional needs. Usually they treat you well and then you respond by loving them. But sometimes they get angry with you and this makes you feel frightened and unhappy. And because they are so big and powerful, you feel helpless. What do you think about that?'

'I don't much like that story,' answered Toad. 'If that was me, I would build a spaceship and escape from those two creatures as fast as I could.'

'Unfortunately, you can't escape. So you are just going to have to put up with the situation and learn how to cope as best you can.'

'In other words,' said Toad, who had caught on to the real meaning of the story, 'I shall have to learn to adapt my behaviour to this particular situation.'

'Well done,' replied Heron. 'You really are learning now. For as you have realised, my story is a parable of infancy. We start our lives with only two, or sometimes only one other person in our life. They are so much bigger than us and we are totally dependent on them. As there is no escape, our only option is to adapt to their every whim. Let me draw a simple diagram to illustrate this.'

He went to the flip-chart and drew a circle and wrote above it, 'The Child Ego State'. Then he divided the circle in half with a horizontal line. In the top half he wrote 'Natural Child'. In the bottom half he wrote 'Adapted Child'. It looked like this:

The Child Ego State

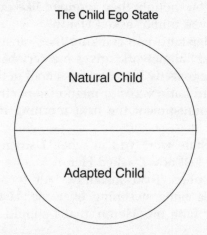

'Now Toad,' said Heron, 'we must finish here. It's been a very full session and I am sure it has given you a lot to think about. So let me give you some homework for our next meeting.'

'Oh no,' said Toad. looking quite anxious, 'not homework! I always hated doing prep. I don't think I shall be able to do any this week. In fact I've just remembered I have a lot of work to do. I will probably have to go up to town. And lots of other things,' he added lamely. There was a long silence.

'Just as a matter of interest,' said Heron, 'how would you analyse what you have just said to me?'

'Well,' said Toad, 'I simply told you why I am unable to do any homework.' He looked uneasy and found it difficult to meet Heron's eye.

'Yes, but how do you think it sounded to me?'

Toad shifted in his chair. 'I don't know really. I merely gave you the reasons why I can't do it.'

'Were they reasons?' asked Heron. There was a long pause. Then Toad spoke.

'Perhaps you thought they sounded like excuses?'

'What do you think?' asked Heron.

'I can understand you thinking that,' answered Toad, 'but the word "homework" gives me very bad feelings. I can remember exactly how I felt at school in the evenings trying to learn Latin verbs or memorise poetry. And then the fear of punishment the next morning if you got it wrong.'

'So what state were you in when I suggested homework to you just now?' asked Heron.

'Child,' replied Toad instantly. 'All those old fears and anxieties came sweeping over me. Is there something wrong with me, Heron, that I should behave like that?'

'No, of course not,' said Heron warmly. 'We all have words or situations which trigger off our childhood feelings. I suppose the most commonly shared word that can do this is "dentist".'

'Oh no, not the dentist!' said Toad, clutching his jaw in mock agony.

'So I will avoid the dreaded "homework" word,' said Heron, 'and instead ask you simply to do some work before our next meeting.'

'What kind of work?' asked Toad, still a little on the defensive.

'Just think about your own childhood. Think about those early days and your earliest memories. And then we can see if our work here throws any light on them. Goodbye Toad. I look forward to seeing you next week.'

6

Toad explores his childhood

Toad found the days following that last meeting strange and unsettling. He found himself remembering long-forgotten incidents in his childhood. Well-remembered events were rehearsed over and over in his mind, and memories of his parents and also of his grandparents were never far away. He went up to the attic and found an old album of sepia-tinted family photographs. These evoked a great sadness in him, not so much because the people in it were no longer alive, but because he featured in so few of them.

He remembered his stern, demanding father, who always gave Toad the impression that he, Toad, did not come up to his high standards and, what's more, never would. He remembered a world inhabited by big, successful men, all of whom, it seemed to Toad, had achieved great things in their different spheres. His paternal grandfather had started the family brewing company, followed by his father when, in turn, he became head of the family. Toad remembered being taken around the brewery as a child and being frightened by the noise and the steam and the smell. He knew then that he would be expected to work in that horrid place, and yet even then he realised that he never could.

He remembered his mother, a quiet person who was dominated by her husband as she had been dominated by her father. He had been an eminent cleric and, eventually, a suffragan bishop. Henceforth he was always referred to as 'The Bishop', even by his daughter. Toad remembered a tall person with an imposing presence and large pectoral cross who always said, in a tone of delighted surprise, 'Ah, little cakes!' when tea was served.

He remembered that at times his mother could be full of fun. Yet Toad felt that she was always conscious of her husband's appraisal and constantly checking for signs of his disapproval. As a result, she would often withdraw her affection from Toad in order to avoid her husband's displeasure and conform to his stricter views. He remembered very few cuddles.

As the day of the next counselling session drew near, Toad felt a mixture of emotions which he had not experienced before. His main feeling was sadness and depression, remembering as he did an unhappy and lonely childhood where there was not a great deal of love or happiness. But even so, he could recall people, rather like 'bit' players, who had made brief entrances into his life, and who unwittingly delineated behaviours and aroused emotions which indicated the 'otherness' of things.

This happened mainly at Christmas time, when a variety of people paid their annual respects and brought presents and hoped to receive dark bottles brought up from the brewery cellars. He remembered an aged aunt with a large black hat secured by enormous hatpins which he assumed must be stuck right through her head. Then there was a strange, jolly person who did conjuring tricks and once, when alone with Toad and to his great amazement, lit his farts. And there was an aged uncle with a gold watch-chain hung across a large stomach, who gave Toad a sovereign and squeezed his thigh in a very horrid way.

And underlying all these memories which came unbidden into Toad's mind, there was growing a strong yet impotent anger. Impotent, because he wasn't sure who he was angry with or what he was angry about.

The result was that he began to feel guilty about feeling angry! For he knew in his heart of hearts, although he would probably not tell this even to Heron, that he was extremely angry with his parents. This anger, however, presented him with problems which he was finding difficult to resolve. Presumably, his parents had done their best for him when he was a child and here he was now, in a beautiful house which he had inherited from them. They had also made sure he was more than adequately provided for. To make it even more difficult, both his parents had been dead for some time! So just as Toad had found it difficult to be angry with them when they were alive, he found it totally impossible now they were dead! But the angry feelings would not go away. Consequently, it was a very emotional Toad who rang the doorbell of the Heronry and took his accustomed seat in the study.

'Good morning, Toad,' said Heron. 'How has your week been?'

'I'm not too sure,' Toad answered quietly. 'I'm frightened that I am beginning to feel depressed again and that worries me, because I thought I was feeling better.'

'What do you think has made you feel like this?' asked Heron.

'I think it is because of the "homework" you asked me to do,' Toad replied. 'I have found it very painful to recall parts of my childhood and that is why I am feeling sad.' And Toad, for the first time in some while, burst into tears.

Heron passed the box of tissues and Toad took one and wiped his eyes. Then he took another and blew his nose vigorously.

After a pause, Heron asked him if he was feeling better.

'Yes,' said Toad. 'Surprisingly I do.'

'You see,' said Heron, 'there is a real and discernible reason for your current sadness. You recalled unhappy times and you responded quite naturally by feeling sad and unhappy. And so you cried. Can you accept that explanation?'

'I suppose so,' said Toad, sniffing, 'but I don't like blubbing like that.'

'I'm sure you don't,' said Heron, 'but if you want to understand more about yourself, you need to get in touch with your feelings and understand them. Otherwise, you deny them, either by ignoring or suppressing them. The result can be rather like an amputation. A vital part of you is severed and effectively you are disabled – to a greater or lesser extent.'

'So it's alright to cry?' asked Toad. 'I remember Father being very strict about it. If I cried, he used to say, "Now stop that blubbing at once or I shall be extremely angry." So of course, I would stop.'

'You have the choice,' said Heron very seriously. 'Will you obey the voice of your dead father, or will you give yourself permission and take your own authority?'

'That seems a very stark way of putting things,' said Toad, looking uncomfortable. 'After all, I'm only - wondering about crying or not. It seems overly dramatic to talk about the "voice of my dead father", don't you think?'

'It may well be,' answered Heron, 'but we are working on dramatic events. From your simple question flow many other important issues that can have a profound effect on your learning and, therefore, on the rest of your life.'

Toad had by now become extremely attentive. His tears had dried up and he was alert and actively listening. 'Go on then, Heron,' he said, 'I'm listening.'

'Good,' responded Heron. 'In that case, I shall take up my teaching role again in order to provide you with more insight into yourself. Do you remember our discussion about the Child Ego State, made up of the Natural and the Adapted Child?'

'I certainly do,' said Toad. 'It has had a profound effect on me and I hoped we were going to talk more about it today. I'm ready for it.'

'I believe you are,' said Heron, 'so here goes. Toad, who were the most influential people in your childhood?'

'That's easy,' replied Toad. 'My mother and father, of course. And in the background, my grandparents.'

'Let us concentrate on your parents first. What sort of a person was your father?'

Toad answered unhesitatingly. 'Stern and upright. I remember him always telling me off about something or other. He would look at me in a very disapproving way and say, "Theophilus, how many times have I got to tell you? Don't do that!" He was always reproving and criticising me. Gradually I grew to accept that he was always right and I was always wrong. And so it seemed logical that he should tell me off.'

'Would he ever hit you?' asked Heron.

'Oh no,' answered Toad. 'There was no need for that. One look from Father was enough! And he would stop being affectionate towards me. Not that he was ever very affectionate. His most severe punishment was to say in an icy voice, "Go to your room and don't come down until you are ready to apologise!"

'I can remember a few occasions when he played with me. But they always ended badly. Perhaps because I was so desperate to be loved by him, I would get silly and do something foolish. I can remember once when this happened, he pushed me off his knee and said to Mother, "I can't stand it when he behaves like this," and walked out of the room. I just burst into tears.'

After a pause, during which Toad's eyes were bright with unshed tears, Heron asked, 'And what of your mother?'

'She was very much under the thumb of Father, but I always felt closer to her than to him. She would occasionally cuddle me, but not much. If I came running to her when Father had been horrid she would say, "Now don't be silly, dear, I'm sure he didn't mean it".

'Because I was her only child, I think she found it difficult to treat me other than as a baby. She embarrassed me terribly at school when she visited me on Sports Days and would insist on calling me "Dear little Theo" in front of the other boys and try to comb my hair.'

'And did things improve as you grew up?' asked Heron.

'Oh no, not at all,' answered Toad. 'For instance, when I was at university and invited some friends to stay, my Father would always find something to criticise whilst Mother would succeed yet again in embarrassing me. She once asked, in front of my friends, if I had put on clean underclothes that day! I can laugh now but I can assure you it was not funny at the time.

'And', continued Toad, 'I'll tell you a story that may interest you. Once, not so long before she died, I plucked up courage and said to her, "Mother, when will you stop treating me like a little boy?" And do you know what she said?'

'I think I can guess,' said Heron, 'but tell me.'

'She said, "I'll stop treating you like a little boy when you stop behaving like one!" There seemed to be no answer to this, so I walked out of the room.'

'That must have made you feel very angry,' said the Heron, after a pause.

'Oh no,' said Toad, 'I never get angry. I'm not the type,' and he smiled weakly.

'So how do you deal with your angry feelings?' asked Heron.

Toad sat up straight and swallowed hard. 'Er, um, what exactly do you mean by anger?'

'Oh, come on Toad,' said the Heron impatiently. 'You know what anger is. How do you deal with it? When were you last angry?'

Toad was thrown into confusion. First, he hadn't been thinking about anger at that moment and, second, he found it difficult to admit to feeling angry at any time. He had always felt as if he would be punished if anyone knew he was angry. The result was that he swallowed his angry feelings and felt extremely guilty instead. But why should Heron suddenly start on this particular subject? Thinking about anger made Toad feel very anxious and he wanted to change the subject. But there was Heron looking intently at him and waiting for an answer. Toad felt he had no choice but to continue.

'To be honest, I'm not sure when I was last angry. Come to think of it, I rarely if ever get angry. It seems so unnecessary and I don't think it's my style.' He smiled a placatory smile.

'Well,' said Heron, 'I think you may find it helpful if

you *did* think about it. After all, you have already agreed that it's one of the basic emotions with which we are all born. Look at it this way, Toad. What do you think happened when you got angry as a child?'

Toad considered this question and remembered his father, tall, stern and forbidding. Behind him, in the shadows as it were, stood his grandfathers, men of character and probity, their very presence spelling out the highest standards of morality. Toad felt that their influence had dominated his life, just as their portraits dominated the Library at Toad Hall.

'I suppose', said Toad, 'that when I remember those early days it's my parents' anger I remember, not my own. I was always being told what to do. Father frequently got angry with me when I misbehaved.'

'So,' said the Heron, 'when a child has stern and critical parents, it must learn to cope with them and adapt its natural behaviour to deal best with that situation. What is such a child likely to do?'

'Does this mean we are back to the Adapted Child State again?' asked Toad.

'Precisely,' answered Heron. 'You will remember that, in the Natural Child, each of us has our basic emotions which are comparable to the primary colours on an artist's palette. But then we must learn to adapt this natural behaviour to our particular circumstances, toning the colours down in order to survive and preserve our personal integrity. This means, amongst many other factors, learning how to cope with anger, the anger of our parents and our own anger.' He paused. 'How do you feel about that, Toad?'

'That's quite difficult to imagine,' Toad replied thoughtfully, 'I'm thinking about your idea of emotions as colours. I am trying to imagine painting a picture which depicts the struggle between the child with its developing emotions and feelings and its parents. They have such fixed ideas about right and wrong and are immeasurably stronger. How does any child survive this battle?'

'You think that growing up must always be a battle?' asked Heron.

'Well, I think it probably was in my case,' Toad answered. 'I think there must have been very strong pressures on me when I was little and I had to cope with critical parents.' He paused and there was complete silence, broken only by the ticking of the grandfather clock in the corner of the room. Then after a while, Toad said in a small voice, 'I wonder how I learnt to cope with all of that?'

'To discover that,' said the Heron, 'let us use our brains and be logical and let me ask you this question. How is a person likely to respond if he is victimised and bullied by someone much stronger than himself and cannot escape?'

Toad thought for a while and then said, 'If such a person is really powerless, he or she must learn to go along with the oppressor. Otherwise I suppose life would be made unbearable.'

'Exactly', said Heron, 'so is it not likely that when *you* were a child, you had to learn how to comply with your parents' strict wishes and demands?' After some time, Toad agreed that that was probably the case.

'So', said Heron, 'what did you have to do?'

Toad thought about this for some time. Within himself, he was feeling sad and unhappy as he remembered those distant times. But, although their source was so far away, those memories and feelings were as alive in his consciousness as if they were happening in the present. However, another part of himself felt alert and challenged and able to think about these matters objectively without being affected by them.

'I suppose,' he said slowly, 'if you are forced to comply with someone, it means that you don't argue with them. You go along with what they say and agree with them.'

'Good,' said Heron. 'I'm going to write this down because I think you are discovering something of great importance.' He went to the flip-chart and wrote the heading 'Compliant Behaviour', and underneath, 'Agreeing'.

'Anything else?' he asked.

Toad pondered for a while. 'I think that as well as going along with my parents' wishes, I always wanted to please them. I'm not sure if I ever succeeded, but I remember clearly wanting them to be pleased and proud of me.' He paused for a while, again deep in thought. 'Perhaps that is why I developed a tendency to show off. They never seemed pleased or impressed with what I did, so I indulged in extravagant and stupid behaviour to try and gain their attention. Is that likely, Heron?'

Heron looked intensely at Toad and realised that, at that moment, Toad's voice and appearance exactly complemented his words. For he looked and sounded, and clearly felt, like a very sad child. This sadness affected the Heron deeply. He sat quietly and tried to share Toad's memories and to experience his sadness, in as far as one person can ever feel what another is feeling. This is called empathy. Toad felt this unspoken support and understanding and it strengthened him to his very soul.

After a while, the Heron said, 'I think you are probably right, Toad,' and then was quiet again, as he sat beside Toad at his pool of loneliness.

'Well now,' said Heron after a while when he judged

the time was right, 'we must press on. Earlier you were saying that you were always wanting to please your parents. Shall I add this to our list of compliant behaviour?'

'Oh yes,' said Toad, his voice stronger now. 'And there's another thing you can write down: "Apologising". I know I do that now and I know I did it as a child. Almost before I had done anything, I would apologise in order to placate Father.'

'Why don't *you* write this up?' asked Heron.

So for the first time Toad took the crayon and added 'Apologising' to the list. Then he turned to Heron and said, 'You know, I am beginning to realise this list describes not only my past, but also my present. What I learnt to do then is curiously close to how I behave now. I don't know if that surprises me or not.'

'I suppose what *is* surprising', answered Heron, 'is to realise just how much of our adult behaviour was learnt in childhood. But when you think about it, it is fairly obvious. The strongest feelings we had as children inevitably become those we regularly experience as adults. Perhaps that was what the poet meant when he wrote "The child is father of the man". And I would like to add one further item to our list, if you agree.'

'What's that?' asked Toad.

'Dependency,' answered Heron.

After a pause, Toad said, 'Are you sure about that? I mean, aren't all children dependent on their parents? Isn't that the natural way of behaving when you are small and helpless?'

'Yes it is,' answered Heron, 'but for most people, the very essence of growing up is to lessen and finally break those ties of dependency and become an independent and autonomous person. Few achieve this totally, some achieve it partially and many remain dependent all their lives.'

'But what has this to do with compliant behaviour?' asked Toad, somewhat cautiously.

'What I mean,' said the Heron, 'is that compliant behaviour can result in someone learning to be dependent as a way of life. In other words, they never really grow up.'

'You mean like me, I suppose,' said Toad, and he started to giggle.

'Yes, I suppose I do,' said Heron, and for the first time, he too started to laugh. It was a rather dry sound, as if he did not indulge in laughter very often. But it was a genuine laugh and it enabled Toad to turn his rather irritating giggles into proper laughter.

'Sorry about that,' said Toad, wiping his eyes, 'but we have been so serious and suddenly it all seemed so ludicrous. I just had to laugh.'

'Please don't apologise,' said Heron. 'It's time we finished anyway and how nice that we can do so on a happy note.' This time, Heron walked with Toad to the door and, as he was leaving, turned to him and said, 'Toad, I believe you are making progress. There is still much to be done but you have set your feet firmly on the path of learning and you can never go back.' And with a friendly wave, Heron shut the door. Toad walked home along the river bank and felt happier than he had done for a very long time.

7

Toad meets the Rebellious Child

In the week before the next session, Toad thought a great deal about his own anger and, on the whole, found that he linked it with feelings of guilt. Apart from his father, the person who had been most angry with him in his adult life had been Badger. Badger, that large, strong animal who, ages ago, had tried to stop him enjoying motorcars and had spoken to him so sternly that he had shed bitter tears of remorse and promised to reform. And a lot of good that had done! Toad realised with a flash of insight that Badger could never be a counsellor – because he never listened. Like all angry people, he wanted to *tell* others what to do and then criticise them for their short-comings.

Toad remembered and relived and reviewed one particular situation with Badger. It had happened some years ago when he had been going through a rather difficult time. He had had one or two nasty car crashes when one day, out of the blue, Badger descended on him with Rat and Mole and proceeded to try to make him change his life.

He remembered Badger taking him into the smoking-room at Toad Hall and giving him the severest of moral lectures, reducing Toad to penitence and tears. But when it was over and the severe Badger became a more kindly father-figure, Toad's natural resilience had reasserted itself.

At the time Badger wanted him to confess his sins to Rat and Mole and publicly admit the error of his ways. Well, of course he wouldn't. Toad remembered the situation perfectly and recalled his exact words.

'No,' he had said. 'I'm not sorry. And it wasn't folly at all. It was simply glorious!' He had added impatiently, when Badger appeared scandalised at his words, 'Oh yes, *in there*, I would have said anything *in there*!'

And so he would. For Toad realised that his apparent penitential response had been, in fact, a defence against Badger's attack. It certainly had not come from the heart, and it did not represent a true change. 'But,' thought Toad, 'there I go again. It's always someone else who gets angry, never me. I wonder why?'

Eventually, the counselling day came round again and Toad found himself once more facing his counsellor in the familiar room at the Heronry.

'Good morning Toad,' commenced the Heron. 'How are you in your spirits today?'

'I am feeling a bit happier, I think,' replied Toad. 'I am sleeping better and taking a keener interest in things. For instance, I have started to take a daily paper again and I really read it. At one time, I just couldn't be bothered to open one.'

'That's very good,' the Heron responded. 'And where would you say you are on our Feelings Thermometer?' He rustled through the flip-sheets and turned up the diagram which he had drawn at their first meeting. It was simply a vertical line with one at the bottom and ten at the top.

'I think I feel at about five or six,' said Toad.

'And can you see where you were at our original meeting?' asked Heron, and he pointed to where Toad had placed his mark all those weeks ago. It was between one and two. There was a pause, which Toad experienced as quite a friendly silence, as they looked at each other.

Eventually Toad spoke. 'Heron,' he said, 'am I allowed to set the agenda for this meeting?'

'Of course you are. I shall be delighted if you do,' answered Heron. 'But in a real sense you have always set the agenda. At each of our meetings, I have always attempted to help you work on those issues which will provide you with the greatest insights and learning. If you are now able to identify these yourself, then we are really making progress.'

'Well,' answered Toad, 'I want to analyse my own anger. Or, more correctly, my lack of it. At our last meeting, we looked at how I had adapted my behaviour to cope with my critical parents and you called this "compliant behaviour".'

'Yes, I remember,' said Heron. 'It's still on the flip-chart. He selected the page headed 'Compliant Behaviour', underneath which was written, 'Agreeing.' 'Pleasing.' 'Apologising.' 'Dependency'. 'I suggested this was how you defended yourself from your parents' anger and aggression. So what is your question, Toad?'

'It's really quite simple, but I can't find the answer. Why *don't* I get angry? That's all.'

'Have you never been angry?' asked Heron.

'Well, never like Badger. When he's angry, he looks stern and severe and his voice gets loud and angry and he points his finger at you. I tell you, he can frighten the life out of me!'

'And you are never like that?' asked Heron.

Toad thought hard. 'I suppose there was one time. That was when my friends and I fought the Wildwooders who had occupied my house. I was so angry I uttered war whoops and went straight for the chief weasel. I whacked him really hard and drove him out, along with the rest of them. But that was a very unusual situation. When it was all over, I felt so tired I couldn't get up the next day until lunchtime. It was very much against my nature. I'm not really a fighter. But I have to say that I am proud of what I did on that evening. In fact, *very* proud.'

'You have every right to be,' said Heron, warmly. 'But I still do not know exactly the issue which is concerning you. Can you state your question more precisely?'

'Yes, I can,' said Toad. 'A couple of sessions ago you said – and I agreed with you – that anger is one of our basic emotions. I recall you said that these basic emotions are like the primary colours on an artist's palette. So my question is, 'if anger is a basic constituent of my behaviour, why don't I get angry?''

'That really is an excellent question, Toad,' said Heron. 'However, like all good questions, the answer is likely to give you possibly painful insights into yourself. Are you ready for this?'

Toad looked steadily at Heron. 'I have gone this far,' he said. 'I can't stop now.'

'Right,' said Heron. 'Perhaps the best way to begin is to use our brains and our reason, even though the question is all about feelings and emotions. Let us start by imagining the following situation. You are being held captive by benevolent despots. They have complete dominion over you, yet at the same time they look after you and take care of you. How would you feel about that?'

'I think I would have very mixed feelings about them,' said Toad.

53

'Exactly! And *that's* what you experienced when you were little. How could you be angry with these kindly despots, your parents, who clearly had the upper hand and on whom you were totally dependent? And whom you loved.'

Toad sat very still, deep in thought. 'It does seem to be a genuine dilemma,' he said. 'So what would have happened when the force of my anger met the apparently invincible power of my parents?'

'It seems to me,' said Heron, 'that there can only be one possible answer.'

'And what is that?' asked Toad.

'You had to learn how to be angry non-aggressively!'

'But that's impossible,' Toad replied quickly. 'Surely, being angry *means* being aggressive, by definition. Isn't it more likely that I learnt to suppress my anger totally?'

'I doubt that very much,' answered Heron. 'Anger is such an integral part of our behaviour that it can never be totally suppressed. Let's use another metaphor, this time from science. Imagine a cylinder of gas which has started to heat up. The pressure is increasing and there is danger of an explosion. What can be done quickly to reduce the pressure?'

'The first thing you could do,' answered Toad, 'and the most obvious, is to open the valve as far as possible and vent the gas to the atmosphere in a great, powerful jet.'

'Quite so,' said Heron. 'And this is just how some people learn to deal with their anger. They release it like a powerful jet of gas, directed at a chosen target, and then resume their normal behaviour. What they forget, or deliberately avoid noticing, is the damage they cause and the adverse effect this behaviour has on their relationships.'

'So anger *is* aggressive, like I said?' asked Toad, anxious not to lose his point.

'Yes, it certainly is in this example and that is what I wanted to illustrate. But now, consider this. Think once again about that gas cylinder getting hot and the pressure building up inside. Is there another way to reduce the pressure, perhaps less dramatically?'

'I suppose if you wanted to be more careful, you could simply open the valve slowly and let the gas seep out over a period of time. Is that what you are thinking?'

'Indeed it is,' said Heron. 'Don't you see, Toad? You are discovering the answer! What you and many other people have learnt, is how to be angry non-aggressively. You adopted ways of letting your anger out slowly and gently, almost imperceptibly, so as not to upset anyone.'

'But how?' asked Toad plaintively. 'I can't remember behaving like that.'

'Well,' said the Heron, 'do you remember ever throwing a tantrum?'

'What, is that really anger?' asked Toad in some surprise. 'I mean, tantrums are really pointless and don't achieve anything.'

'My dear Toad,' Heron said patiently, 'that's just the point. Tantrums are a childish display of anger, often as a response to someone saying "No you can't!" to a child. This makes the child very angry, yet at the same time it feels powerless to be violent or aggressive towards the person who has caused their anger. All it can do is to lie on the floor and kick and scream. When adults do this, it is sometimes called "throwing a wobbly".'

'Hum,' said Toad, 'I suppose I have thrown a few of those in my time. But', he added, 'not recently.' Then he continued, 'You said that these forms of non-aggressive anger were spread over time. A tantrum may not last very long.'

'That's true,' answered Heron, 'although some tantrums can go on for a long time. Let's think of a response that can last for hours and even days.'

'Like what?' asked Toad.

'How about sulking?'

'Sulking?' repeated Toad. 'I never thought of sulking as a way of being angry.'

'Well, I believe it is,' replied Heron. 'Sulking is sullen, morose behaviour where the sulker is unusually quiet. I think, Toad, that of all the Adapted Child's behaviours sulking is the best illustration of using time to reduce the force of anger. It is usually a child's response to authority, when they can't get their own way. In adults, it often happens for the same reason, perhaps when someone has lost a power struggle. Sulking is essentially a loser's response to the more powerful winner.

'It achieves just what we have been talking about. It reduces the force of anger by releasing it gradually at a very low level of intensity. And this of course reduces the aggression.'

There was a long silence as they both thought about this. Toad was beginning to realise that more and more of his behaviour originated from his Adapted Child. Heron was trying to recognise how far Toad was understanding these issues, and asking himself whether he, the Heron, was doing too much of the talking.

Eventually Toad asked, 'Are there many other ways in which a child learns to be angry?'

'I'm sure there are hundreds,' Heron replied. 'When you think about it, each of us must adapt to the particular circumstances of our childhood. It is like a great mosaic of behaviour, with all the associated feelings and emotions.'

'So can I ask you how *you* analyse them?' Toad asked.

'Certainly,' answered Heron. 'Let me draw you a diagram.'

And this is what he drew:

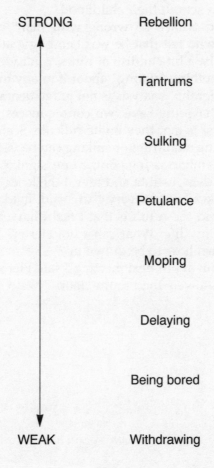

How a Child Releases Its Anger

STRONG   Rebellion

Tantrums

Sulking

Petulance

Moping

Delaying

Being bored

WEAK   Withdrawing

Then he continued, 'Of course the point is – and I know you are beginning to realise this, Toad – that all these behavioural strategies are, in effect, defence mechanisms developed in our childhood to protect us from the dangers we perceived then, real or imaginary. When we see adults sulking and throwing tantrums and moping about and saying they are bored, we may wonder if their behaviour is appropriate or whether they are compelled, yet again, to act out their childhood.'

'Well, and what's so wrong with that?' asked Toad petulantly, who felt that he was being 'got at' by Heron. 'We can all be a bit childish at times, can't we?'

'There's nothing "wrong" about it in any moral sense,' answered Heron. 'Analysis is not judgemental. But these kinds of behaviours have two consequences, both negative. The first is that they invite ridicule. Seeing a grown person having a tantrum or sulking can be very amusing, as well as embarrassing. But, more significantly, these behaviours demonstrate and reveal the loser.'

'That makes me feel very bad,' said Toad. 'We do all this work and the result is that I feel I have been stupid for a lot of my life. What can I do, Heron? When am I going to learn how to be grown up?'

'How about at our next meeting?' said Heron, and with a smile he showed Toad to the door.

8

A surprise visit from Mr Badger

It was about teatime and Toad was watching cricket on the television. He had always enjoyed the game and, although he no longer played, he was the president of the village team and took a keen interest in all the county matches. He was just thinking about making himself some tea when the front doorbell rang.

There were no longer any servants at Toad Hall. A woman came in to clean twice a week and a number of the larger rooms were permanently shut. Toad lived mainly in the kitchen, which was warm and snug, and he had the television in the small breakfast-room which adjoined it, which had lovely views over the gardens and down to the river. He kept the front door closed and always used the back entrance.

So when the bell rang he got up quickly and walked down the long, dark corridor, pulled back the bolts, unfastened the chains and finally opened the large, iron-studded door. There, to his great surprise, stood Badger!

'Good afternoon, Toad,' he said briskly and walked through the doorway and strode purposefully down the hall.

Toad, initially speechless, shut the front door as best he could and scurried after him, apologising for the state of the house and saying, 'Why didn't you let me know you were coming?' and generally blabbering on and feeling a complete fool.

Badger, who had been a great friend of his father and knew Toad Hall well, was about to open the doors of the drawing-room. But Toad got there first. 'I don't use this room much nowadays. Come on down here.' The fact of the matter was that Toad hadn't used the drawing-room in years. It was dusty and musty and cobwebs festooned the curtains.

Toad took Badger into the breakfast-room and, having picked the newspaper off the floor and shoved his slippers under the table, offered Badger a seat. He hovered about feeling very anxious and ill at ease.

'Can I get you anything, Badger?' he asked. 'A cup of tea? A slice of cake?'

'No, thank you,' Badger answered. 'I never eat between meals. And Toad, do you think you could turn that television off? I can't hear myself think.' Then he added, 'It's a bit early to be watching the box, isn't it? I never put it on before six. Just for the news. There's never anything worth watching.' Toad immediately switched off the offending set.

He perched himself on the edge of a chair and tried to make conversation. 'It's beginning to get warmer, don't you think? Some of the crocuses are out.'

'Only crocuses?' asked Badger in surprise. 'You should see my daffodils. Masses of them!'

Poor Toad, his daffodils were only just emerging. He was filled with shame for being such a poor gardener.

'But you do go on, Toad,' said Badger sternly. 'It would be nice if you could listen for a change.'

'Sorry,' said Toad automatically. He sat down meekly and waited for Badger to continue.

'Now look here, Toad,' he began, 'the reason I am here is because there is something that must be discussed. I know that you have not been yourself lately and have been out of circulation. But the rest of the world moves on, you know. Things can't stop just because you are not feeling well.'

'No, of course not,' said Toad. 'Silly of me to think so.'

'So', continued Badger, 'I am concerned that something should be done. I am sure it is what your father would have wished.'

'Oh, certainly,' Toad murmured. 'I'm sure he would.' But he didn't have a clue what Badger was talking about.

'You do know to what I am referring, don't you, Toad?'

'Well, not exactly,' answered Toad. 'Could you spell it out for me a little?'

'Surely it's obvious. It's about you being a governor of the village school.'

'Yes, I am,' said Toad. 'I haven't attended many meetings recently because ... ' He paused. 'Because I have been unwell. But I mean to start going again soon.'

The village school was small with only two classes, but it had educated several generations of villagers. Now that people were moving away into the nearby town, the number of pupils was falling and there was even some talk of closing it down. Toad, however was committed to its continuation and had spent many hours on the committee, trying to raise funds and maintain standards.

'Well, that's just it,' said Badger. 'Everyone knows that you haven't been to the meetings recently and there are some big issues coming up.'

'Yes I know,' said Toad, 'and I mean to go to the next

one.' He had in fact just received the minutes of the last meeting and was about to write to the vicar, who was the chairman, to tell him that he would definitely be attending.

'But you probably won't be well enough by then, will you?' asked Badger. 'You're still looking a bit peaky. What does that counselling fellow say? Depression, wasn't it? Funny, I don't think I have ever been depressed in my life. Too much to do, I suppose. No time to sit and brood.'

Toad felt that Badger was looking at him accusingly. He started to feel angry, but this quickly changed to feeling miserable. He felt that Badger thought he was malingering, and he wished he could pull himself together and be more like him.

'So I've had a word with the vicar,' Badger continued, 'and he agrees with me. There's no need to worry yourself.'

'What has he agreed to?' asked Toad, apprehensively.

'Why, to me taking over your place as a governor. Not that I really have the time,' Badger said sternly, looking at Toad over his half-moon glasses. 'What with the Bench and the District Council, there aren't enough hours in the day. But one must do what one can.'

'But I am still on the committee,' said Toad, feeling a bit stronger. 'You know I am.'

'Yes, but if you resign for health reasons', answered Badger, 'there need be no election and the vicar said that he would co-opt me on to the committee. So I thought, Toad, that you could write your resignation letter now and I will take it straight over to the vicar. Save you the trouble of posting it.'

Toad was in a turmoil. He was feeling so angry, he would have liked to punch Badger on the nose. How dare he! How dare he go to the vicar behind his back and try to get him removed from the school council! What a nerve! He really enjoyed being on the school committee. He felt that he had something to offer and he always enjoyed organising the school's summer fête on the lawns of Toad Hall.

But then, he thought, Badger might be right after all. Perhaps he ought to resign and let him take over. He would certainly bring tremendous energy to the task. But, thought Toad, he would bring other things as well. He would bring his temper and his intolerance and his ability to get people's backs up. I suppose that's the price you have to pay for Badger, he thought perceptively. But is it too high?

'Well, Toad, are you going to write it?' asked Badger impatiently.

Toad didn't know what to do. Badger seemed so strong and confident and he felt so small and uncertain.

'Perhaps I need a day or two to think it over,' he said in a small voice. 'After all, I have been a governor for some time and I think I would miss it.'

'Yes, Toad, you probably would for a few days. But we must not be sentimental. Remember, it's what's good for the school! We must not let our personal feelings get in the way of that.'

'Oh no, of course not, Badger,' answered Toad. 'I hope I'm not being selfish.'

'I'll tell you what,' said Badger, 'why don't you have a think about it and telephone me later this evening? That will give me time to contact the vicar and fix everything up.'

'I think,' said Toad, summoning up all his courage, 'I think that I shall need longer than that. I will phone you tomorrow evening.' Toad remembered that he was going for a counselling session next morning and he needed Heron's help.

'Very well,' answered Badger. 'You were always indecisive, Toad. I didn't get where I am today by being indecisive! See a problem, come up with a solution, make a decision. That's how I deal with things.' He rose from his seat.

'Don't bother to see me out, Toad. I can find my own way. And Toad,' he added, 'I should get to bed early if I were you. You're looking peaky. You should take more care of yourself. Look after Number One, that's what I always say.' And with that, he was gone.

Toad had just enough strength to pour himself a stiff brandy and soda before he collapsed on to the settee.

9

After Badger's visit

Toad could hardly wait until the next day, when it would be his counselling session. He was hopping mad. (Appropriate for a toad, he thought, in a lighter moment.)

'Just wait until I tell Heron,' he said to himself. 'He'll never believe it! He won't credit it that Badger came to my house, uninvited, and tried to get me to give up my school governorship. Badger had better not show his face here again in a hurry or it will be the worse for him! I'll show him!'

However, it must be understood that this anger and frenzied activity were going on *within* Toad. Such feelings and such anger! But there were no external signs by which the outside world would have known just how strongly he was feeling.

By the evening his anger had subsided and he was once again in his usual unhappy state of mind, feeling sad and miserable. 'Badger's right after all,' he thought. 'He would make a much better governor than me. He's got such drive and determination. They probably only made me a governor because I live here at the Hall and they can use the garden for their summer fête. That night, he slept badly and woke early.

When he went to the Heronry on the following day, he was feeling low and miserable. Heron ushered him in and said, 'Morning Toad, and how are you feeling?'

'Bloody awful,' answered Toad, who did not usually use bad language but felt this last trace of anger blow over him like the tail end of a hurricane.

'Why don't you tell me about it?' asked Heron.

And so Toad told him the sorry tale of Badger's visit and how he had wanted Toad to resign from the school committee.

'So how did this make you feel?' asked Heron.

'Terrible,' answered Toad. 'I don't seem to be of much value to myself or to others. I've just about definitely decided to resign and send my letter to the vicar. It will be best for everyone.'

Heron remained silent for some considerable time. It was not that he didn't understand Toad's situation. He understood it only too well. But he was uncertain which path of learning to pursue. Eventually he spoke.

'Toad, I have to congratulate you. You play a very good game.'

Toad looked up, bemused. 'Game? What game? I'm not playing a game.'

'I suggest that you are,' answered Heron. 'You play a very good game of PLOM.'

'Plom? What on earth is that?' asked Toad.

'PLOM stands for "Poor Little Old Me" and you win it every time. Or lose. It all depends on your point of view.'

'I really don't understand what you are talking about,' said Toad peevishly. 'I am not playing a game. I've told you in all honesty about a very unpleasant situation which has befallen me and you say I am playing a game with you?' Toad looked at Heron reproachfully.

'"Honesty" is an interesting word,' said Heron.

'Are you saying that I'm dishonest?' said Toad, beginning to feel angry. After all, his family motto was 'Guard Thine Honour'.

'Yes, I think I am,' said Heron surprisingly, 'but not in the usual sense of the word. I think you can be dishonest with your *self*. Why do you keep getting into situations where you end up looking stupid and someone gets the upper hand and you feel like a poor little child again? Is it just wretched bad luck, or do you in some way collude in the process?'

'What does "collude" mean?' asked Toad.

'It means a secret agreement. I use "collude" to mean that you secretly or unknowingly cooperate with others to create your own unhappiness. And that's why psychological games are played. And the losing is in the winning,' said Heron enigmatically.

'Now look here, Heron,' said Toad strongly as he tried to resist these ideas, 'there was no "collusion" as you call it. I never knew Badger was going to call. Or ask me to resign. And I want to remain a governor. It all came out of the blue. So how could I have cooperated with him, secretly or otherwise?' Toad was clearly very upset.

Then Heron made what was the closest to an apology Toad had ever heard from him. 'I'm sorry, Toad,' he said. 'I obviously have not made my point well or else you are not yet ready to explore this particular idea. You feel that I am accusing you and nothing could be further from my mind. So may we leave that point and come back to it later?'

'If you say so,' answered Toad rather huffily. 'But I shall want to hear more about these so-called games. I take it that there are others you think I play?'

'Yes, I think there probably are,' replied Heron. 'But if you are feeling so defensive, you will not be able to analyse them now. I think we should move on.'

There was a pause, as Toad realised that he was feeling extremely strongly about the things Heron had just been saying. Yet he wasn't sure why.

'Alright,' said Toad, 'but you may be right. I felt very hot under the collar when you said that about colluding and wanting to make myself unhappy. It seems so stupid that I should try to make myself miserable.'

'Look, Toad,' said Heron, 'some of the ideas which arise in this work can initially seem silly or illogical or even frightening. And those ideas that are most likely to provide the deepest personal insights are those most likely to be strongly resisted.'

'Why is that?' asked Toad.

'Because they threaten our equilibrium the most,' answered Heron. 'They are the ideas that are most likely to lead to personal change at a deep level. And that is often painful, as I think you are discovering. When we look at ourselves, we do not always like what we see. To move from where we are now to where we would like to be must inevitably involve changes in our behaviour and our attitudes. To achieve this requires hard work, courage and determination. So you can see, Toad, why you might resist opening a door that could lead on to such a difficult path.'

'But it could also lead to great understanding,' said Toad quietly.

'Of course,' said Heron, 'and that is why we are working together, travelling on the same path.' There was a long pause as they sat together in a companionable silence.

'Shall we move on now?' asked Heron eventually. 'You

had been telling me about Badger's visit and how he made you feel. So let me ask you this question. What kind of state do you think he was in when he called on you?'

'He certainly was not in the Child Ego State, that's for sure,' said Toad. 'It's hard to believe that he was ever little. He always reminds me of my father.'

'Well done, Toad. I believe that you are exactly right. In fact, Badger was in the Parent Ego State.'

'And what exactly is that?' Toad asked.

'When we are in the Parent State, we behave like our parents. Remember, they were the first people we ever experienced. So their influence on us is immeasurable. The Parent State contains all the values and morals we have learnt from them since birth. It contains our standards for living and enables us to say what we believe to be good or bad, right or wrong. These values originated from our parents, who were the main influence on our behaviour. Their words and actions moulded our early years and inevitably influence the rest of our lives.'

'So do you think that Badger's parents would have been stern moralists and that is why he behaves as he does?' asked Toad.

'It's very likely,' answered Heron, 'but remember this, Toad. We are never simply a clone of our parents. Whilst they have enormous influence on us, our own personal uniqueness ensures that we are not just copies of our mothers or fathers, but individuals in our own right.

'So', he continued, 'what other behaviour would you expect to see in someone who is in their Parent Ego State?'

'The way they look, do you think?' asked Toad. 'I'm thinking of my own father. He could look very stern and displeased at times.'

'Right,' said Heron, 'and how did he sound?'

'Angry. He could either be quiet and cold and icy, or he could be loud and frightening. I'm not sure which frightened me most.'

'And can you think of other examples of people you have met who were in their Parent?' Heron asked.

Toad thought for a bit. 'Yes, I have come across other people like that. Certainly some of the masters at my school.' He paused. 'When you start to think about it, you come across examples of it all the time. For instance, I went to the cricket ground the other day to see how the preparations were going for the Saturday match. Our groundsman, who's a surly old so-and-so, was painting the white lines on the crease. I went up to him for a chat and asked him how he was getting on. He looked me in the eye and said, "I was doing alright until you came along!" I felt very uncomfortable.'

Heron smiled. 'That seems like a very good example. Any others?'

'Yes, there is one that comes to mind,' Toad replied. 'I can still feel angry when I think about it. I went to the dry-cleaners the other day to take a number of my bow-ties to be cleaned. They had got rather grubby, soup stains, that sort of thing. The lady behind the counter took one look at them and said, "You don't want dry-cleaning. You want a bib!" The cheek of the woman.'

Heron smiled. 'Once again,' he said, 'I think you are on to something important. Let's write it up.' He went to the flip-chart and wrote the heading 'The Parent Ego State'. Underneath he drew a circle and divided it in half with a vertical line. In the right half he wrote 'Critical Parent'.

'Now Toad,' he said, 'what words would you use to describe someone in their Critical Parent State?'

'Well, I think we have mentioned them already,' Toad

replied and he took the crayon and wrote 'Judgemental', 'Angry', 'Severe'. 'I suppose there are lots of others?' he said.

'I'm sure there are,' answered Heron, 'but I think these encapsulate the Critical Parent.'

Toad sat down and looked at the words which he had written. After a while he said, 'Heron, there's something I don't quite understand.'

'Can you put it into a question?' asked Heron. 'That usually takes the learning forward.'

'I'm not sure that I can, initially,' Toad replied. 'You see, what you have just told me about this Parent Ego State has really opened my eyes. For instance, it helps explain Badger's behaviour so well. When he came round to my house, almost everything he said was critical or judgemental. No wonder that he reminds me so much of my father! Knowing what I know now, I can almost predict what Badger will say when we next meet. And how he will behave.'

'Excellent,' said Heron. 'You are clearly developing your emotional intelligence.'

'I am?' asked Toad in surprise.

'Certainly,' said Heron. 'Intelligence is not just a matter of IQ. We need EQ as well.'

'Well,' said Toad, 'I don't feel very intelligent about my next question. Which is this. Where's *my* Critical Parent? You said that everyone has got one and it derives from what our parents said to us and how they treated us when we were little. It certainly helps to explain the way Badger, and other people, behave. So what about me? Where's mine? I honestly don't think I've got one. I hardly ever get angry. That's really true, Heron. I don't get angry with people. I don't tell people off. I don't shout at them or criticise them. In fact, it's usually the opposite. I see the best in them and encourage them. It makes me a sound a bit weak, I know, but that's how I am.'

There was a long pause before Heron spoke. 'Toad, are you ready for some more personal learning? I mean learning at a deep level?'

Toad looked steadily at Heron. 'Yes I am,' he said, 'but it hurts sometimes, you know. I am getting many new insights, but I don't always like what I discover.'

'I know, I know,' said Heron sympathetically, 'but remember what they say, "No gain without pain".'

'I find that kind of saying particularly annoying,' answered Toad with some spirit. 'You usually find it written on calendars with pictures of seagulls and rose-coloured clouds. Trite. Or tripe.'

'Be that as it may,' answered Heron, in what Toad thought was a slightly pompous manner, 'let us try to find the answer to the problem you have posed. Perhaps we can clarify it by writing it down.' He went to the flip-chart, found a fresh page and wrote the following:

Does Toad have a Parent Ego State?

Then he said, 'Now let's write down some of the para-meters of the problem.' And he wrote:

1 Everyone has a Parent Ego State.
2 There seems no evidence that Toad has one.

Then he turned to Toad and said, 'So what should be our next question?'

'Clearly, the next question must be', answered Toad, 'why haven't I got one?'

'I think there is a more logical question than that,' said Heron.

'What is that?' asked Toad.

'We could ask, "How does it operate?"'

Toad thought for a moment. Eventually he said, 'I don't understand. I thought you agreed with me that I don't have a Parent State. So how can it operate?'

'I don't agree that you don't have one. In fact,' said Heron, 'I believe you have a very powerful one. The question is, "how does it work?" It's clear that it operates in a very different way to Badger's.'

'You've got me really confused,' said Toad. 'I don't know where I am.'

'I think confusion is often the first stage in the learning process,' said Heron. 'It happens when fixed boundaries begin to unfreeze. You start to be confronted with new data that challenge existing beliefs and behaviour. It can be the beginning of creativity, the anxiety that drives the process of change.'

Toad looked unconvinced by Heron's explanation. 'It don't feel like that,' he said grumpily and ungrammatically.

'So let's try thinking about this problem in a different way,' said Heron. 'Let's think of this Parent State as more like a judge, who is seeking to accuse someone, find them guilty and then, quite logically, punish them. Does that make sense to you, Toad?'

'It certainly does,' he said.

'Do you think that Badger behaved like a judge yesterday?'

'Oh, definitely,' said Toad. 'That's just how he was and I felt like the prisoner at the bar. I can speak about this from experience, you know. It's terrible to be found guilty. But it's even worse to *feel* guilty!'

'So who do *you* judge, Toad?'

'That's just the point,' said Toad irritably. 'I don't. I'm not that kind of person.'

'Toad,' said Heron, 'may I invite you to think again and ask yourself the question: who do you judge?'

There was a long, long silence. Then Toad said in a small voice, 'I think I see what you are getting at. Do you mean that I judge myself?' Heron sat quietly and said nothing. After some time, Toad spoke. 'Then I suppose I find myself guilty and condemn myself. Is that it?'

'There can be no stronger criticism than self-criticism. And no harsher judge than ourselves,' answered Heron.

'Oh dear,' said Toad. 'Do you mean we can punish ourselves?'

'Severely,' said Heron, 'including torture and, in extreme cases, execution. But the problem is that, even if the sentence is light, it can be imposed for life.'

'So what can I do?' asked Toad. 'I've got a lot of life in front of me. I don't want to keep punishing myself, if that is what I do. I'd like a bit of happiness. What can I do, Heron? Can you help me?'

'It may sound a little stark, Toad, but it is you and only you who can help yourself. There are lots of questions that you should consider. For instance, can you stop judging yourself? Can you be kinder to yourself? And perhaps the most important question of them all. Can you start to love yourself?'

Toad sat still, completely motionless. After a while Heron said, 'Are you alright Toad? It's time to go.'

'Yes,' he replied, 'I'm alright. But you've given me so much to think about, my mind's buzzing. I feel quite light-headed.'

'So be careful going home,' said Heron, 'and I will see you next week.' Then he added, 'Toad, do look after yourself.' And Toad walked slowly down the path and through the gate.

10

Lunch at Rat's house

The last session with Heron left Toad feeling rather desolate. He understood the concept of the Critical Parent when it was applied to other people, Badger especially. But when he applied it to himself, the thought that he was criticising and even punishing himself was unnerving.

Yet at the same time, he was aware that there were changes happening to him. Deep within himself, he was feeling stronger. He found that he was able to consider these very emotional and threatening ideas more rationally. He was less emotional when he viewed himself objectively, and this enabled him to understand himself better and to learn. Yet, intellectually, he felt that there was still a piece of the puzzle missing.

He understood just how much of the time he was in his Adapted Child State. And it was beginning to dawn on him that he had the ability, or even the need, to criticise and punish himself in the same way his parents had done when he was little. He remembered something that Heron had said about collusion, 'a secret or unknowing cooperation with others'. Could you collude with yourself to condemn yourself? And without even knowing you were doing it, even unconsciously?

These were difficult ideas for Toad to handle, especially when they involved his very self. They flitted through his mind like shadows, and seemed equally impossible to capture and examine. What was the way forward? Heron kept on about understanding and learning, but where was it all leading? For the first time since he started to work with the Heron, he wondered how much longer the counselling would last.

But at the same time, Toad was beginning to feel more energetic. One morning, he found himself walking down the garden path that led to the dry boat-house where a number of racing skiffs were kept. He examined them and found one that appeared to be in good condition. He carried it to the water's edge, fetched the oars, carefully climbed in and started gently to paddle the boat upstream. He didn't do at all badly. He had always rolled and splashed a good deal but this time he consciously restrained himself and after a while returned. When he got out, he was panting and his back was aching but he felt good. 'I really enjoyed that,' he said to himself. 'And that deserves a beer!' So he went and had one.

Later that week, he received an invitation to lunch with Rat and Mole. Since the beginning of his depression, they had left him on his own. This was for a number of reasons. The first was that they were a little embarrassed by Toad's initial behaviour and were uncertain how to cope with it. And, second, like all sick or wounded animals, Toad had simply wanted to crawl away and be left on his own and he had clearly signalled this.

But now things were different. For a start, the weather was improving. The sun was getting warmer every day and, up and down the river bank, boats were being painted and varnished ready for summer. Word had got around that Toad was on the water again and not looking too bad. But more than all of that, Rat and Mole had missed him. So they invited him to lunch.

As Toad walked along the river bank to Rat's house, he felt very fragile. It was as if the suit of armour he usually wore was removed. His senses, especially his sight, seemed to be particularly acute. The colours of the grass and the trees were unusually vibrant and he thought that never before had he realised there were so many different shades of green. He felt in touch with things and alert to his surroundings. As he walked, he found that he was checking over his feelings in much the same way as a pilot checks his instruments before take-off. Although he was slightly apprehensive about meeting his friends again, on the whole he was feeling good. If Heron asked me where I was now on his Feelings Thermometer, he thought, I would say eight.

When he arrived, his friends gave him an extremely warm welcome. He was given the best chair by the fire (it was still chilly indoors), and Mole shoved cushions all around him to ensure that he was comfortable.

'Oh Toad, it's so good to see you,' said Mole. 'We've been so worried about you.'

'Yes, we have,' said Rat gruffly. He couldn't show his feelings quite as easily as his friend. 'We certainly have missed you. Sherry?'

Toad was offered a small glass of dry sherry and tried to sip it slowly. He could never understand how anyone could make these tiny glasses last so long. He was essentially a brandy-and-soda man and, when he drank sherry at home, he tended to use a wine-glass.

'How are you chaps?' he asked. 'You're both looking well. Anything much happening on the river bank? Have I missed much?'

'No, not much,' answered Mole. 'You know how it is in the winter. Things can go very quiet and this year it was too cold to go out much.' Mole paused. 'But do you notice anything, Toady? I've spent a lot of time decorating this room. Do you like the wallpaper? It's a William Morris design called "Willow Boughs".' Toad looked around and realised that the room was in fact looking very different from when he had last seen it. The walls were papered with a swirling pattern of thin brown willow branches laden with green and yellow leaves. Mole had whitewashed the ceiling and the whole room, with its old oak furniture and glowing fireplace, had an air of solid comfort and sensible values.

'Excellent,' said Toad. 'How well you've done it, Mole. I only wish Toad Hall looked half as smart,' and he started to feel a bit dejected.

'Now then,' interrupted Rat, 'how about some lunch? Nothing fancy here you know. We live quite plainly.'

Mole was about to add, 'Not like you do at Toad Hall,' but he saw how Toad was feeling and kept quiet.

The lunch was plain but good. Rat had made a thick onion soup with croutons. Then there was a Stilton and plenty of fresh crusty bread and butter and pickles. They finished their meal with a plate of the best kind of apples, Cox's Orange Pippins, and all of this was served with a frothy jug of beer.

Soon tongues were loosened and Toad began to feel at ease, almost like his old self. He found himself laughing at one of Rat's anecdotes and responding with one of his own. Then Mole asked if he had seen Badger lately. 'We haven't seen him for ages.'

'Well, strangely enough, he called on me only the other day,' replied Toad.

'Called on you!' exclaimed Rat. 'Good heavens. He

must think the world of you, Toad. I've never known Badger to call on anyone before.'

'Well, it wasn't quite like that,' said Toad, and he started to tell them about Badger's visit and how he had wanted him to resign his school governorship so that he could take it over.

'Well I'm blowed!' said Mole when Toad had finished the story. 'What a nerve! Badger's got many good points and he's very energetic. But he can be very arrogant. What a nerve!'

'Yes,' agreed Rat, 'but you haven't told us what you finally decided to do.'

'Haven't I?', asked Toad. 'Well, I thought about it for a long time. I even discussed it with Heron.'

'Is that your counsellor?' interrupted Mole. 'How's that going?'

'Oh, not too bad,' said Toad. Then he continued, 'I had finally decided to resign. I just felt I couldn't go against Badger any longer. He's so strong and so sure of himself. But then I thought, Why should I? Why should I have to agree with him? Why shouldn't I do what I want to do? To be honest, I felt quite angry with him.'

'So did you go to see Badger and tell him?' asked Mole with great interest.

'No, I decided not to,' said Toad. 'I felt that if I saw him I would be bound to lose. Rather childish really, I admit, but true. So I wrote him a note instead, saying that on further consideration I would not resign because I was feeling a lot better. If he felt like it, he could put his name forward in September when I come up for re-election and we will see what happens then.'

'Well done,' said Rat warmly. 'I think, given the circumstances, you handled that extremely well.'

'Yes, you certainly did,' agreed the Mole. 'I'd say that you won.'

'Do you really think so?' asked Toad, feeling strangely pleased. 'I felt worn out by the end of it. I felt I had been fighting a battle which was not of my choosing. Anyway, it's over and done with now . . . I hope,' he added *sotto voce*.

After some more chat, Toad said that he must be getting back. Rat and Mole said they would go with him as they needed the exercise. So the three companions walked back to Toad Hall. There Toad thanked them for lunch and they agreed to meet up again soon.

'Perhaps a rubber of bridge?' suggested Rat, who played a sound hand and had taught Mole the basics of the game.

'We would need a fourth,' said Mole.

'Not Badger,' said Toad strongly.

'No, I was thinking of Otter,' answered Rat. 'Anyway, we'll leave it for now and get in touch. 'Bye.' And off they went.

As they were walking home, Mole said to Rat, 'Well, what do you think?'

'About what?' asked Rat, whose mind was on other things.

'About Toad, of course. Don't you think he's changed?'

'Yes I do,' said the Rat. 'But it's hard to put your finger on it.'

'He listened more,' answered Mole. 'That's what it was. He listened and, what's more, he seemed genuinely interested in what we had to say. Usually you can hardly finish a sentence before he comes crashing in. If I'm honest, he seemed nicer. And quieter. Not so tiring.'

'Yes, I know what you mean,' agreed Rat. 'He used to be a bit of an ass. Always boasting and full of himself. But

I suppose his breakdown (this had become the accepted way to describe Toad's situation) has knocked the stuffing out of him. But I was surprised to hear his story about Badger. Toad would never have stood up to him in the past. What a difference!'

'Yes, I agree,' said Mole. 'But', he added wistfully, 'I think Toad has lost his sparkle.'

11

Toad meets the Adult

'So', said the Heron at their next counselling session, 'how are you feeling today?' Toad not only expected this question but was in fact eager to answer it.

'I'm feeling much better,' he said. 'I am certainly happier in myself and I have much more energy.' He told the Heron about starting to row again and how he had been to lunch with his two friends.

'That's excellent,' replied Heron, 'but Toad, have you thought why these changes have come about?'

'I'm not sure,' he replied, after a long pause. 'It's very hard to understand what's going on inside your own head. But I certainly feel stronger. It's difficult to explain. There are still times when I get those familiar feelings of sadness and worthlessness. They are still inside me somewhere, but they no longer take centre stage. I seem to be able to push them to one side, and I don't feel so dominated by them.'

'I am delighted to hear that,' said the Heron. 'You are clearly developing your self-insight and emotional intelligence. But let me ask you this.' He looked hard at Toad. 'What ego state were you just in when you answered me then?'

Toad thought. 'Well,' he said, I certainly was not in my Parent Ego State. And I know that I wasn't in my Child.'

He paused. 'Recently I've been thinking that there ought to be another ego state, in which you are neither behaving like your parents nor feeling like a child. One in which you are more grown up. More like yourself at the present moment, if that makes sense.'

'It certainly does,' said Heron enthusiastically. 'There *is* such a state. And you have discovered this for yourself. Well done!'

'Have I?' asked Toad in some surprise. 'What is it called? The Grown-up State?'

'Not quite,' said Heron. 'It's called the Adult and it completes the trinity of the ego states. The three of them are Parent, Adult and Child and these three states describe the structure of your personality. We can draw this very simply.' He took up the crayon and was about to draw on the flip-chart, but Toad interrupted him.

'May I?' he asked. 'I know just how to draw it.' And this is what he drew:

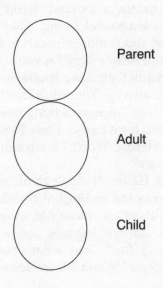

'Can you tell me more about this Adult State?' he asked.

'The Adult Ego State', replied Heron, 'is the rational, unemotional way we have of behaving. It enables us to deal with the reality of what is happening in the here-and-now.'

'And what exactly does that mean?' asked Toad.

'It means', replied Heron, 'that it is the state in which we can plan, consider, decide and act. It is the state in which we behave rationally and logically. When we are in this state, we have all our knowledge and skills available for immediate use. We are not driven by the old voices of our parents or swamped by the feelings of our childhood. Instead, we can consider the present situation and decide what we want to do now, based on the facts.'

'So does that mean that this Adult State is more important than the others?' asked Toad.

'No, not exactly,' answered Heron. 'All of the states are essential for successful living. They have evolved over hundreds of thousands of years and so each must be important and have a survival value. But what we *can* say is that this Adult State has a special importance.' Toad was listening attentively. 'The Adult Ego State is the only state in which we can learn something new about ourselves.'

There was a long pause. Then Toad said, 'Are you sure about that, Heron? Won't I learn something when I'm in the Child State?'

'No,' said Heron, 'I don't think so. In the Child, you will experience the feelings of childhood, both good and bad. You will act out those old situations and feel those old feelings. But nothing new can be learnt.'

'I see,' said Toad, 'but what about when I'm in the Parent Ego State? Won't I learn something then?'

'Again, I think the answer is "No", but for different reasons,' Heron replied. 'When you are in the Parent, you are essentially being either critical or nurturing. Either way, you are repeating in words or behaviour the beliefs and values you learnt from your parents. You want to demonstrate them and tell them to others. It is a state of certainty and so there can be no place for new knowledge or ideas. The old ones reign supreme. That is why no one ever changes their mind through an argument. They simply become more entrenched in their views.'

Toad paused. 'So are you saying that I can only learn something about myself if I am in the Adult Ego State?'

'Yes,' answered Heron, 'I believe that is correct. For it is only then that you can consider new facts or evaluate your behaviour or, and this is extremely difficult, listen to another person's view of you without immediately dismissing it.'

'So why have I found it so difficult to learn?' asked Toad. 'If what you say is true, why didn't you just get me into my Adult State and tell me what to do? It would have saved so much time.'

'I don't know if you are being serious or not,' Heron replied, 'but I will work on the assumption that you are. First, no one can force another person to be in their Adult State. You can only encourage them, as I am encouraging you all the time. But I can't force you. Only you yourself can decide to behave in that way.' Heron stopped and looked intently at Toad.

'And second?' asked Toad quickly, to relieve the pressure he was beginning to feel.

'Second,' said Heron, 'I don't *know* what you ought to do. The main aim of this counselling is to enable *you* to discover for yourself what you ought to do. I can facilitate the process, but only you can decide.'

'Yes, I recognise that,' said Toad slowly, 'but why is it so difficult?'

Heron thought for a while and then said, 'It is difficult because it requires hard work and conscious thought. When you are in the other two ego states, it scarcely requires thought to act like a parent or a child. We behave unthinkingly because we know what to do and say. It's rather like being in a play.'

'How do you mean?' asked Toad, who enjoyed amateur dramatics.

'It is as if we take on a favourite role which we know perfectly. We know our lines and we know our movements. For instance, take the role of Angry Man. The Angry Man knows how to be angry so well. Given the right situation (and isn't it strange how often this occurs for him?) he is word-perfect. Without a thought, his voice achieves the right tone and level, he automatically selects the appropriate words and his whole stance demonstrates his angry feelings. In a word, he plays the Angry Man to perfection and, this is the point, without even thinking! It is as if his whole life has been a rehearsal for this current performance. And because he has played it so often, it gets better each time.'

Toad looked quite anxious. 'Are you saying that angry people get angry deliberately?' he asked. 'They choose that role?'

'Of course,' answered Heron, 'or why else would they do it?'

Toad paused. 'Well, it might be that someone has made them angry,' he said.

'You've made a very important point, Toad, and it's worth looking at it in greater detail. I don't believe that anyone can *make* us feel anything, unless they use force and coercion. In the last analysis, we *choose* our own feelings. We choose to be angry or we choose to be sad.'

'Oh, come on now,' interrupted Toad. 'No one in their right mind is going to *choose* to feel sad or miserable. That just doesn't make any sense.'

'I know it sounds unlikely,' answered Heron, 'but look at the alternative. How could anyone reach into your mind and force you to feel anything? Now that really *is* impossible. They may well influence you or persuade you. But in the end, you decide and choose what you will feel.'

Toad looked perplexed. 'Are you saying that people choose their own mental suffering and torment? I really can't believe that.'

'I agree that it is difficult to accept,' said Heron.

'Bloody impossible, if you ask me,' muttered Toad under his breath.

Apparently Heron did not hear. 'Well perhaps "choose" is not quite the right word,' he answered. 'We don't choose how we feel in the same way that we choose to have another chocolate. But we make these kinds of choices unconsciously. It's more like a conditioned reflex.'

'What's a conditioned reflex?' asked Toad.

'A conditioned reflex is an automatic response to a certain stimulus. You must have heard of the famous work of Pavlov, when dogs salivated at the sound of a bell which they had learned to associate with being fed. The poor beasts became conditioned to doing this. They could not stop themselves. It became an automatic reflex.'

'I suppose it's not so different from the doctor hitting your knee when your legs are crossed and your foot jumps automatically. You can't stop yourself.'

'Exactly,' said Heron enthusiastically, 'that's a perfect example of what I mean. Except that we are talking about emotional behaviour. Because of our past experiences, we learn to respond to certain situations automatically and without thought. You could say that, like those dogs, we can't avoid doing it.'

'But that's just what I've been saying,' intervened Toad. 'If we can't avoid doing it, it can't be our fault. You can't blame me if I get depressed. That would be extremely unhelpful.' He paused. 'And very unfair.'

'So, Toad,' answered Heron after quite a long silence, during which Toad felt extremely uncomfortable, 'who do you blame for your recent unhappiness? Who made you feel so bad?'

Toad stopped and started to think. Something inside warned him that he was going down the wrong track, but he was feeling very animated and could not or would not stop.

'In the first place, it was Badger. And then Rat. And Mole, too, to some extent. I told you how horrid they all were to me when I returned from. . . .' he paused, 'when I returned from being away. And then you have helped me to see that it was the way my parents treated me when I was growing up that has caused me to be the way I am. I know that they probably weren't aware of what they were doing, but I have to blame them. There's no one else. I *do* blame them. I have had a rotten life.' And Toad wept bitter tears of anger. 'It's not fair,' he said. 'It's just not fair.' And he went on sobbing.

Heron sat still. He did not push the box of tissues closer. He just sat. Eventually he spoke, and in a way that commanded Toad's immediate attention.

'Toad,' he said, 'you have come to the cross-roads. You can't go back. So which way will you go?'

'I'm not sure what you mean,' said Toad, drying his eyes. 'You make it sound as if I have to make some sort of choice. Is that right?'

'It is,' answered Heron. 'The choice is this: how much longer are you going to blame other people for your own unhappiness?'

'But you know the alternative,' said Toad petulantly. 'You want me to blame myself. And I won't do it.'

'That is not the option I am suggesting at all,' said Heron. 'Blaming is done from the Child Ego State, which seems to be your favourite position. But what might be an appropriate response in your Adult State?'

Toad tried to get his brain to work, but he was full of conflicting feelings and subconsciously he knew he was on the edge of a very significant piece of self-discovery. 'I'm not sure I know,' he said.

'Instead of blaming, how about taking responsibility?'

There was a long, long silence. 'I'm not sure I follow you,' said Toad eventually, in a quiet voice. 'You mean, I should take responsibility for my own actions?'

'And for your own feelings,' said Heron. 'That's a very adult thing to do, and no doubt very difficult. But it does have one enormous advantage over blaming others.'

'And what's that?' asked Toad.

'It means that you can start to do something about it. If you take responsibility for yourself, you realise that you can take your own authority. Consequently, you realise that you have the power to change your situation and, more importantly, change yourself.'

'But what about my parents?' Toad asked. 'What can I do about them? How can I get my own back?'

'Are they alive now?'

'No,' answered Toad. 'They have been dead for some time.'

'Then there's only one thing that you can do,' Heron replied.

'And what's that?' asked Toad anxiously.

There was a pause. 'Forgive them,' answered Heron.

Toad started to speak. He wanted to ask Heron why he should forgive them. They had made his life miserable. Why shouldn't he get his own back and hurt them in the way they had hurt him? He was beginning to feel angry with both Heron and with his parents. They merged in his mind into one hated object. He felt that he was on the edge of a terrible rage, which if he released it, could do untold damage. It might even kill someone. He sat there, his heart beating faster and he felt extremely hot. But as always, those strong feelings of anger began to evaporate leaving him feeling tired and miserable.

Whether Heron was aware of Toad's emotional turbulence is hard to say. After a while, he said gently, 'I think we should finish now,' and walked with Toad to the front door. As they stood on the doorstep, Toad turned and said, 'Heron, are you really interested in me?'

'What a strange question to ask!' answered Heron. 'I am extremely interested in you and I am trying to understand all that has happened to bring you to this very moment in time.'

'Yes, I know that,' said Toad, 'but do you understand all that I have been through? Do you understand my life as a whole?'

'Well, put like that, I don't suppose I do,' answered Heron. 'I know bits of it, especially about your childhood. But I don't know your story from beginning to end. Do you want to tell it to me?'

'Yes I do,' said Toad, 'very much indeed. I would like to tell you my complete story. I've never told it to anyone before. It's not that it is so amazing. In fact, it's rather commonplace, I suppose. I just want the opportunity to tell someone everything that has ever happened to me. Just once. So that you can understand. '

'Very well,' said Heron. 'Let's do that at our meeting next week. You shall be the storyteller and narrate "The True History of Toad" to me. How about that?'

'Thank you,' said Toad. 'Goodbye.' As he walked down the path and through the gate, he was already planning what he would say.

12

The true history of Theophilus Toad

One week later, Toad was sitting opposite the Heron, waiting to begin his narrative. He was feeling quite excited because he realised that never again would he have this opportunity to recount his complete life-story to an attentive audience.

'Where should I begin?' he asked.

'Wherever you like,' replied Heron.

'Well, my earliest memory is sitting on the sand under an umbrella, feeling sad. We always went on holiday to Cornwall where we had a large, dark house called Moss Terrace. You went up steps to get to it and it had a wonderful view over the harbour. But it was always an unhappy time. My father only came down at the week-ends and, as an only child, I was alone with my nanny and my mother. Mother was always so busy that I spent a great deal of time on my own – feeling sad.'

'But what about the rest of your family?' asked Heron.

'If you want me to start right at the beginning, then I have to begin with my paternal grandfather, Cornelius. He started the Old Abbey Brewery which is brewing to this day. Unfortunately, it is now owned by the National Beer Company and makes lager. Ugh!

'He was, I suppose, typical of his generation, hard-working, paternalistic to his employees and very moralistic to his family. My father told me that in those days, every man received a turkey at Christmas and two pints of beer every lunchtime. I remember as a very small person being taken around the brewery offices by Grandfather and being addressed as "Young Master Toad". I also remember him pointing to me and saying to the head clerk, "Here's the future Chairman", and I felt scared.'

'Why was that?' asked Heron.

'Because, even then, I knew that I did not want to work there!'

'Why?'

'Because I was frightened of Grandfather. He was big physically and I could feel that he was very powerful. We lived in a large house in the village but he lived at Toad Hall. You can't imagine what it was like, visiting him and Grandmother at the Hall. There were maids and servants and cooks and an army of gardeners and once a year at the regatta, the house was full of visitors for days at a time. One year, I was told, the Prince and Princess arrived by boat and there was a wonderful lunch on the lawn. But I'm afraid it's not half so grand now.' Toad stopped and a large tear rolled down his cheek.

After a pause, Heron spoke.

'What about your father?' he asked.

Toad blew his nose and then continued. 'I always felt that my father would have liked to be more like Grandfather than he actually was. So I think it made him stricter and more autocratic towards me. When I think of him now, and he's been dead these past twenty years, I can still feel his disapproval. I was never the toad he wanted me to be!

'Thomas, my father, was hard-working and achieving and driven by the Protestant work ethic. I think he always felt the burden of inheriting, not only the brewery but also the position of Chief Executive. This was especially true when Grandfather retired, but remained Chairman. I am sure that Father felt, although he was Managing Director, that he was standing in Grandfather's shadow and he had to prove himself in everything he did.'

'So how do you remember him?' asked Heron.

'As stern and disapproving. I always wanted his love and attention, but I never got it. One of Mother's recurring phrases was, "Not now, Theo," (my Christian name is Theophilus, although not many people know this), "can't you see that your father is busy?" Father had a way of saying, "Theophilus!" that made me quake in my shoes.'

'So what about your mother?' asked Heron.

'Fortunately, Mother could be much more loving and I remember some cuddles from her. But never in front of Father. When he was present, she would be more severe with me and this would make me feel guilty and anxious. I never knew what I was supposed to have done to cause her sudden change in attitude. But she had quite a sense of fun and I remember her playing with me, especially dressing up and singing. Once, Father came in unexpectedly and she stopped immediately. To this day, I can still experience that same anxiety and guilt for no apparent reason.'

'And what about her parents?' asked Heron. 'Do you remember them?'

'It's funny you should ask me that,' said Toad, with a little more animation than he had shown hitherto. 'Her father, my maternal grandfather, had a very strong influence on my early life. He had been a Fellow at a college in Cambridge and then became rector in a country parish nearby, where he became very involved in the Mission to the South Seas. Rather to everyone's surprise, he was made Suffragan Bishop of Blewbury and became quite famous for his preaching. I often think that I may have inherited a little of his skills of oratory.' As the Heron did not respond to this remark, Toad continued.

'He was always referred to as "The Bishop" even by Mother, although we very rarely saw him, but I remember once that he came to our church to preach a missionary sermon. Mother strongly supported his work and we had any number of missionary boxes in our house, shaped like straw huts, with a slot in the roof in which you put your pennies. I was told that the money would help the Bishop to start schools and hospitals in the South Seas. But more excitingly, the money would also help build a boat to sail around the islands.'

'But what has this to do with the Bishop's visit which you remember?' asked Heron.

'I'm coming to that,' said Toad. 'When the Bishop came to preach his sermon, he gave us a tour in spirit of the whole boat, as yet unbuilt. He asked a blessing on every piston, spar and stanchion and, at the end, we sang "For those in peril on the sea". I was so enthralled that I think that was where I got my lifelong love of boats and boating.'

'What about your schooling?' asked the Heron.

'That's another matter,' answered Toad. 'When I was seven, I was sent to a prep school in Brighton called Galleons where I was deeply and continuously unhappy. Luckily the Head was quite a decent sort, gentle and slightly shell-shocked from the war. On the whole, we were not treated badly, but there was never enough food. But there are two things that I can remember to this day.'

'What are they?' asked Heron.

'First, the loneliness and sadness of leaving home at the start of every term. And second, the excitement of coming home at the end of term and then finding it all so disappointing and unwelcoming.

'At thirteen, I went to St Endymion's, a minor public school in Yorkshire which was centred both structurally and organisationally around the school chapel. The school was founded on the principles of muscular Christianity, and this left me out of breath and out of sympathy. I never liked it and I found team games agony. There were frequent references to "the Bishop, your grandfather" who I discovered was on the board of governors. It was made clear to me that he would not have been happy with much of my behaviour.'

'So was it all pain and grief, Toad?' enquired the Heron.

'Oh no, not at all,' replied Toad with some vigour. 'I enjoyed singing in the choir, and one of my triumphs was taking the female lead in the end-of-term operetta. I started to play golf and got my handicap down to twelve. But much more importantly, I discovered that I could make friends.

'I could always make people laugh and, with Father's allowance, I could also treat them at the tuck shop. I was known as "Good old Toady" and I liked that. Come to think of it, I still like it. Perhaps that is why I like Mole so much.'

Toad paused and thought for a minute. The Heron did not interrupt. Then Toad continued.

'I worked well enough to be able to stay on in the sixth form which, in many ways, was where I began to find myself. That was where I first began to wear a bow-tie and I can still remember Father's intense disapproval when I wore it at home. For the first time, I felt real satisfaction at his reaction. If he was going to disapprove of me, I thought at least I would give him something to disapprove of! I've worn one ever since.' He fiddled self-consciously with the dark blue polka-dotted bow-tie he was wearing.

'I also started a dining club at school called "Puddings" and I was the founder-president. We used to meet out-of-bounds in the neighbouring village, and this was the start of my lifelong interest in food and wine. I also started to get a reputation as a bit of a bohemian, and bought records of Stravinsky and Berg. I think some of the masters were quite impressed, but my taste has changed now. I prefer Schubert.'

If these somewhat surprising revelations affected Heron, he did not show it, other than by uncrossing and then recrossing his long, thin legs. 'So then what happened?' he asked.

'I went up to Cambridge. Somehow I managed to scrape through the Latin entrance exam and got one of the places allocated to my school. Initially they wanted me to read theology. Imagine! But this was quickly changed to history, which I hated.'

'So why did you agree?' asked the Heron.

'Oh, it's easy enough for you to talk,' answered Toad peevishly. 'But all my life people have made decisions for me. Can't you see that?'

Heron replied that he could not, but would Toad like to continue.

'Well, in spite of that, I really enjoyed myself at Cambridge. I met up with a crowd of fellows, perhaps not quite the friends my father would have wished, and we formed the "Aeolian Poetry Society". Once a week we met in each other's rooms for breakfast and read out our poems and drank white burgundy. As well as this, I was always good at punting and in the summer term it was all picnics and hampers up to Granchester.'

'What about your work?' asked Heron.

'I was just coming to that,' said Toad, 'but it's a bit painful, even now.' He paused and thought deeply. 'Because of all these other activities, my academic work was suffering. To be honest, it was really non-existent. I constantly missed tutorials and I would send round a charming note of apology to my tutor, together with a bottle of vintage port. Nothing was ever said until my final term.'

'What happened then?' asked Heron, leaning slightly forward in his chair.

'Well,' said Toad, looking very uncomfortable, 'I have never told anyone this before. I was summoned to the Master's study and he read me the riot act. He said some things that were quite hurtful and, to my mind, unnecessary. Once again I was compared unfavourably to the Bishop, who, it turned out, had been a Fellow at the college.

'But perhaps the unkindest cut of all was when the college Chaplain, who had actually attended one of our Aeolian breakfasts, sent me a note inviting me to ponder on a certain biblical text which I have never forgotten.'

'What was it?' asked the Heron, now quite obviously interested.

'It was Daniel 5:27. It refers to Belshazzar's Feast and what the Mystical Hand wrote on the wall.'

'Well, come on then,' said Heron, now very interested. 'What did it write?'

'It wrote "Mene, Mene, Tekel and Parsin". I knew this story from childhood and we used to say that it meant "Eeney, Meeney, Treacle and Parsnips". But I had forgotten its true meaning.'

'Oh, come on, Toad,' said Heron impatiently. 'What does it really mean?'

'It means this,' said Toad. '"You have been weighed in the balance and found wanting"!'

There was a long pause, during which Toad fidgeted uncomfortably and the Heron looked into the middle distance. Then, when Toad seemed more composed, Heron said, 'So what happened then?'

'The last thing anyone in college wanted to see was an undergraduate fail his finals. So I was put on what was called a "Special" course, and my final exams consisted of only one paper, "The Life of Nelson". As I had a month to swot for this, I finally passed. My father was so surprised and pleased when I told him that I had been awarded a "Special" that he increased my allowance! But I knew that dark clouds were forming on the horizon and that the storm was about to break.'

'Talking of breaks,' said the Heron, 'I suggest that we take one now,' and he left the room. Soon after, Toad heard the sound of running water and Heron reappeared.

'So, where were we?' asked Heron. 'Ah yes, I remember. The storm was about to break. Would you like to carry on, please?'

'Well, what I was going to say was this,' continued Toad. 'For a long time, Father had been dropping hints, not very subtly, that I should take over the brewery. The thought appalled me, all that smell and steam and having to start work at seven-thirty! I don't usually get up until ten! One minute he was persuading me that it was my duty to do it and that the business must remain in the family. This would make me feel very miserable and inadequate and I would say that I didn't feel up to it. Then he would round on me, call me a waster and say all manner of unpleasant things about me and my friends and how the last thing I was capable of doing was managing a business!'

'How did all that make you feel?' enquired Heron.

'Well, what do you think? I felt very unhappy and I used to spend a lot of time in the local hotel cocktail-bar and get home the worse for wear.'

'So what happened then?'

'A Cambridge chum let me know that they were looking for a junior master at my old prep school in Brighton, Galleons. I applied and, rather to my surprise, I got the job. I got on well with the boys and I was supposed to teach them everything. But the school prided itself on a strong naval tradition, so my special knowledge of Nelson proved to be invaluable. In fact, I became quite popular and, to be honest, I enjoyed it. My nickname was "The Odious Toad", but I think that it was said affectionately.'

'A man amongst boys and a boy amongst men,' said the Heron quietly.

'What was that?' asked Toad.

'Nothing much,' replied Heron. 'What happened then?'

'Well, I was there for about a year when, out of the blue, I got a telegram saying that Father had died from a heart attack and that I was to return immediately. Apparently he had just sold the brewery and I think that the stress involved in this killed him. Mother, who had a whole heap of shares, went off to live with her sister in the West Country and I found myself inheriting Toad Hall and a great deal of money.'

'So you felt happy?' asked the Heron.

'No,' replied Toad vehemently, 'I felt very unhappy and very inadequate. Toad Hall is a very large place with a banqueting-hall and very extensive grounds. I suddenly found that I had to look after all of it, which included cooks, servants and outside staff. In the evenings, I would walk around the rooms, many of which I had never entered before, and feel very alone.

'But gradually I began to build up my life. I started to invite a few friends in for lunch. I hate eating on my own. Then I got very interested in boating and made friends with Rat and later with his friend, the Mole. I found that other people started to invite me into their organisations. Perhaps it was simply that I was now Toad of Toad Hall, but I was invited to become the President of the village cricket club and also of the local British Legion. I was elected onto the parish council and became a church warden, just like my father.

'Father had set up the Toad Hall Housing Trust to provide housing for local people. I was one of the trustees and all of these activities took up quite a few days and evenings every month. Gradually, I found myself caught up in a network of civic and social relationships.'

'So you felt that your life was becoming a little more purposeful?' asked the Heron.

'A little,' replied Toad, 'but when there wasn't much happening, the old feelings of sadness and isolation would come over me and I would have a bad couple of days.'

'So how did you react to these feelings?' asked Heron.

'I was always looking for something I could excel at, something that would make people look at me and say, "Look at Toad. Isn't he wonderful?" First came boating. I bought some really fine skiffs and worked very hard. My ambition, which I have never told anyone before, was to enter for the Diamond Sculls at Henley, but somehow I never got any better. Even the ducks used to laugh at me. And then one day I woke up and thought, "To hell with boating!", and I have never rowed again. Until the other morning, that is. My boathouse is full of lovely boats that are rotting away.

'Then came caravanning. I had seen some pictures in a magazine and I bought one of the best. It really was beautiful, a brand-new gypsy caravan, painted canary yellow, picked out with green and red wheels. And it came fully fitted. I can see it in my mind's eye now. Little sleeping-bunks, a little table that folded up against the wall, a cooking-stove, lockers, bookshelves, even a bird-cage with a bird in it, and pots, pans, jugs and kettles of every size and variety.' Toad stopped and sat with a far-away look on his face as he remembered those golden days.

'It so happened that on the day after it was delivered, my friend the Rat came round for lunch with Mole and they agreed to come with me on a wonderful holiday. Or at least, that's what I thought it would be!

'Oh dear me,' sighed Toad, tears beginning to roll down his cheeks. 'If only I had known then what I know now. It all seemed so innocent and exciting at the time. It was like the world must have been before the Fall. We were all little children again. Or at least *I* was. It seemed that the church clock stood at ten to three and there was honey still for tea.' He paused. 'And then everything seemed to go wrong. . . .' Toad's voice trailed away into silence as he sat there sobbing and remembered how evil had entered his world. Heron remained silent.

Eventually Toad wiped his eyes and sat up straighter. In a small voice he said to Heron, 'I suppose you know what happened to me after that?'

'Yes I do,' replied Heron. 'I've read about it like every-one else. I'm afraid that part of your life is forever in the public domain.' He paused and then said, 'Shall we stop there? I think that you have given me a full and detailed story of your life and I hope you feel that because of this, I can understand you better.'

'Yes, I do,' said Toad, who was beginning to cheer up a little. 'And be honest, Heron, it's quite an interesting story, isn't it?'

'It is extremely interesting,' answered Heron, 'but the point is, what can you learn from it?'

And with that question, Heron closed the meeting and escorted Toad to the door. As he was about to leave, Heron said, 'By the way Toad, whatever happened to the bird in the cage in your caravan after the accident? I've often wondered.'

'Mole took it home and looked after it,' Toad replied. 'As a matter of fact, he's still got it. Nice creature, Mole.' And Toad walked down the path thinking that for most of his life, he had felt as caged as that poor bird. Would he ever escape from his past and find freedom? He knew how Heron would answer that: he would say, 'That's a good question, Toad. What is your answer?' How infuriating! But as he walked home, Toad started to work out his response.

13

The continuous creation of Toad's familiar world

Being able to tell Heron all about his life in the form of a narrative had affected Toad more than he cared to admit. It had been an enormous relief to tell another person about his experiences, without being laughed at or rejected. Here was his life, for better or for worse, in which he was neither a great saint nor a great sinner, just Toad. What pleased him most was the way Heron seemed to be genuinely interested in all of it.

As he narrated it, it had given him the opportunity to see his life in the round. He began to realise some of the influences which people and events had had on him over a long time. He started to see trends in his behaviour and the ways in which one experience led to another. Previously, when he had recalled past events in his life, they had been isolated flashbacks with apparently little connection. Occasionally he had recalled and considered longer periods in his life, such as his imprisonment, but then he was only too keen to drive away those unpleasant thoughts and think about something else.

But now he was beginning to gain the capacity to recall without condemning. He made connections between events and looked at them objectively without feeling guilty. Gradually, he was beginning to understand why certain things had happened in the way they had and to realise the implications. In other words, Toad was reflecting on his own behaviour and beginning to learn from it.

He was looking at his life strategically and finding that some of the ideas gained from Heron were extremely useful. The idea of life as a stage was nothing new, but it was new to think that maybe he had a 'life-script' which he was acting out whenever possible. It was even more disturbing to think that maybe he unconsciously engineered situations to enable that script to be regularly used. Did that mean that, somewhere in his unconscious (he could use this word now without embarrassment), there may even be a 'life-plot' with a particular kind of ending and towards which unknown forces were driving him?

If these ideas were true or, as Heron would say, 'had truth in them', what sort of play was he in? Sometimes it seemed that he was in a comedy where he was the object of scornful jeers and laughter, and where, try as he might, he could not change the script. But lately he had begun to realise that there might be another way of living, where instead of following a predetermined script a person might be able to live without one, making it up as he went along, so to speak. That could be quite frightening, because how would you know what to do or what to say without a script? At least this removed the problem of thinking and deciding for yourself. Without it, what would you say after you say 'Hello'?

On the other hand, it could be very exciting to recognise that each new moment presents unique possibilities and challenges. Toad decided that this was what was meant by being authentic, responding genuinely to the demands of the present moment. It could break the chain of cause and effect, which might well extend back to childhood, and provide the freedom to be who you really are, with the true self emerging unshackled from the past. He decided that he would like to be a bit more authentic in his life and the way he lived it.

On the night before the next counselling session, Toad had a disturbing dream. He dreamt that he was in an aeroplane, wearing his old motoring togs of cap, goggles and gauntlets. He was the passenger in the rear open cockpit and the pilot was in front. Suddenly, the pilot turned around and grinned horribly at him, showing all his teeth. It was Badger. 'You're on your own now, Toady,' he shouted and, with that, he jumped out and Toad saw his parachute open.

Toad was in great alarm and anxiety because he had never flown a plane before, but somehow he managed to land it in a field. He climbed out and ran away, just as the plane exploded in a fireball. He woke up, covered in perspiration, feeling frightened and yet at the same time exhilarated, because he had managed to land the plane himself and escape death.

The next day, Toad went for his counselling session with Heron. After the preliminaries, Toad started to tell Heron the thoughts which had started to flow from their previous meeting, when he had related his life-history.

'So you see, Heron,' said Toad, 'I have started to think of my life much more as a whole and about my script and my own personal drama. But what I can't quite see is, where does it all come from? Is there a way of understanding how my script came to be written? Because I'm not sure that I like the role I am cast in and, so far, I have not enjoyed the play very much. Perhaps if I understood how it arose, I could change it. I prefer plays that have a happy ending.'

Heron smiled. 'I understand just what you mean, Toad. And it would be nice to be in a play which managed to avoid any of "the slings and arrows of outrageous fortune". And we might explore how to cope with these sorts of situations later on. But, as I understand it, you would like to explore the origins of some of your basic attitudes and behaviour. Is that right?'

'That's exactly right,' replied Toad, 'but I'm not sure how to proceed.'

'Well, you won't be surprised if I tell you that in order to understand your present, you must look at your past. In fact, to your earliest beginnings. From your birth to about age four or five, everything that happened to you made the greatest impression on you and your development. It could scarcely be otherwise. This involved how you saw yourself and how you saw others. As a result, you have formed your particular view of the world and, as far as you are concerned, that's the only way you can see things. You have spent the rest of your life living in your world and seeing everything from that viewpoint.'

Toad thought for a bit and then said, 'Do you mean that it's like an astronomer taking one particular view of the heavens and basing all his ideas and calculations on that one limited and restricted view?'

'Exactly,' said Heron, 'but we are talking about a psychological view of your personal world, taken from deep within you. You might say, a view taken from your very soul.'

'So what did I see?' asked Toad.

'Each of us sees a different world, depending on the nature of those early experiences,' answered Heron. 'And sometimes those worlds are so different, with such different beliefs and assumptions, that they can only be reconciled by bloodshed in later life.'

'I don't understand that,' said Toad. 'Surely we all live on the same planet Earth. There can't be such differences between us, can there?'

'But you know there can, don't you, Toad?' replied Heron. 'Compare your childhood with, let us say, that of a child brought up in the slums of Brazil. Or, an even more telling case, an English child, in a family much poorer than yours, but who was dearly loved and cherished.' Toad's eyes glistened with unshed tears.

'Each of these children will have formed its own unique and very different view of the world. Don't you see?'

'Yes, I understand that,' said Toad. 'For instance, if we had all taken photographs of one particular day in our childhood, they would be very different, wouldn't they?'

'Yes, they would,' answered Heron. 'But remember, we are not just talking about the physical world. We are talking about your inner, psychological world of feelings and emotions which were formed through the experiences of those early years. Those first years of life are so powerful and vibrant for every child that they result in the formation of their unique view of the world. In other words, the world out there becomes my world in here,' said Heron, patting his chest. 'Whatever attitude you formed about life then, will have influenced your behaviour and happiness ever since. And it will continue to do so for the rest of your life. That is' – and here Heron looked directly at Toad – 'unless you decide to change.'

'Oh, come on,' said Toad, 'surely I've not based all my

life just on those early years? I mean, I had hardly begun to live by then and lots of things have happened to me since. I have had some very exciting and frightening adventures and I know they have had a profound effect on me.'

'There can be no way round it, I'm afraid,' said Heron. 'Every life must have a beginning, a middle and an end. And the beginning must obviously influence those later stages. As a consequence, you form a view of the world based on your initial experiences.'

'I'm still not entirely clear about this "view of the world" idea,' said Toad. 'Can you explain it more precisely?'

'Yes, I think I can,' answered Heron. 'It is as if in your early years, say between four and five, you try to answer two questions.'

'And what are those?' asked Toad suspiciously.

'The first is "What do I think of myself? Am I OK?" The second is "What do I think of others? Are they OK?"'

There was silence as Toad pondered these existential questions. 'Who asked me those questions?' he said at last.

'Life itself,' answered Heron, 'and in particular, your experience of it.'

'But what exactly does "OK" mean?' asked Toad.

'"OK" can stand for any specific good and "Not OK" for any specific evil.'

'So how might I have answered those questions?' asked Toad. 'I might have said "Yes" to one and "No" to the other.'

'That's right,' answered Heron. 'And because you can say either yes or no, there can be four resulting combinations. Let me write them down.' And he went to the flip-chart, took up the crayon and wrote this:

1 I'm OK; you're OK
2 I'm OK; you're not OK
3 I'm not OK; you're OK
4 I'm not OK; you're not OK

'Do you understand that, Toad?' Heron asked.

Toad looked uncertain. 'I'm not quite with you,' he said with a puzzled look. 'Can you make it any clearer?'

'Perhaps it will help if I draw a diagram,' said Heron, and he proceeded to draw this:

Life positions

I'm OK

I'm OK; You're not OK	I'm OK; You're OK

You're not OK ——————————|—————————— **You're OK**

I'm not OK; You're not OK	I'm not OK; You're OK

I'm not OK

Heron continued. 'On this diagram, you can see that the quadrants define these four Life Positions that I have just described. What we have to do now is to examine them and tease out their meaning.'

'But why is this so important?' asked Toad impatiently, moving around in his seat, which was a sure sign that he wanted to challenge what was being said. 'Even if it *is* all true, and I can't see how you can possibly know this, what does it matter *now*? After all, I may have taken up

110

one of these so-called "positions" when I was three or four but now that I am . . . ' he paused, 'now that I am older, it seems quite irrelevant.' Interestingly, Toad never gave his precise age and Heron never knew it.

'My dear Toad,' said the Heron patiently, 'the whole point is that these are *life* positions. Once we decide on these attitudes as children, we hold on to them for the rest of our lives. They become the very fabric of our being. From then on, we construct a world which confirms and supports these beliefs and expectations. In other words, we make our life a self-fulfilling prophecy.'

'Hang on a minute,' said Toad, 'you're losing me again. I thought that a prophecy foretold what was going to happen. Like Isaiah and Hosea and those other old prophets in the Bible.'

'That's right,' said Heron. 'But in this case, *we* control events to make sure that our prophecy will come true. We make sure that our world confirms our expectations.'

'Well, how on earth can we do that?' asked Toad in some surprise. 'We don't know what will happen in the future so I can't see how we can influence it. You never know what's going to happen, even when it seems a certainty.' Toad's experience of attending race meetings over a number of years had provided him with proof of this.

'I think it would be helpful if I were to introduce a new idea here,' said Heron and before Toad could answer, he went to the flip-chart and wrote 'Inevitable Consequences'.

Toad frowned in concentration. 'Can you give me an example of what you mean by that?' he asked.

'Certainly,' replied Heron. 'What are the inevitable consequences of drinking too much alcohol?'

'Getting drunk, I suppose,' said Toad who, on occasions, had taken one too many.

'Anything else?' asked Heron.

'Feeling awful the next day. Having a hangover. Is that what you mean?'

'Precisely,' said Heron. 'These are the inevitable consequences of getting drunk. So you could say that it is a way of determining the future. If, for instance, you believe that your life is unpleasant and unfriendly, getting drunk today is one certain way to confirm this miserable expectation tomorrow. In other words, you create a self-fulfilling prophecy.'

'But surely', said Toad, 'having a few drinks with friends and then having a thick head the next day doesn't require such a serious explanation, does it?'

'No, of course not,' said Heron. 'What I am describing is behaviour which is repeated regularly over a long period. Perhaps over a lifetime. This kind of behaviour is then called a game. As a matter of fact, that particular game is called "Alcoholic".'

'A game!' exclaimed Toad. 'It doesn't sound much like a game to me.'

'It's a psychological game,' replied Heron. 'It's the kind of game referred to in that famous book *Games People Play*, where a hundred games are named and described. And the inevitable consequence of playing these kinds of games is that the players end up feeling bad and unhappy.'

'Could you give me another example of a game?' asked Toad.

'Easily,' replied Heron, 'but before we continue, I need you to answer this question. What is the most important idea that we must examine next?'

Toad tried to think, but this question had come at him so quickly that he was confused. 'Just a minute,' he said. 'I'm not quite with you.'

'Oh, come on, Toad, I haven't got all day,' said Heron impatiently. 'It's obvious what the answer is. Think, man, think!'

Toad felt that he was back at school being asked a question to which he did not know the answer.

'Oh you are a duffer, Toad,' said Heron. 'Haven't you been paying any attention to what I've been saying?'

Toad mumbled something about not being sure quite what the question meant when, suddenly, Heron burst out laughing.

'Well, Toad, did you enjoy that game?'

Toad looked quite sullen. 'I don't think it's fair to ask me that kind of question suddenly. I didn't know what to say. You have made me feel quite stupid.'

'I'm sorry about that,' said Heron, 'but that was the game.'

'Was it really?' enquired Toad, still in a huff. 'I hope you realise that I didn't enjoy it. What was this so-called game called?'

'It is called "Guess the Word in My Head". Teachers have played this with their pupils for years and of course they are bound to win. It ensures that the student feels stupid, as you did just then, and it ensures that the master triumphs over ignorant pupils and feel superior. I must admit', added Heron, 'that I didn't realise that you would be such a strong player. But I think I have made my point.'

'So you are certainly not talking about "fun and games", are you?' said Toad. 'That felt quite vicious.'

'No, definitely not. Every game is basically dishonest and the outcome is always dramatic, rather than merely exciting. What seems on the surface to be dealing with factual issues is, in fact, motivated by something much more devious. Games are played at two levels. There is the social level, where things appear to be open and honest. And there is the psychological level, where the motivation is covert. That's where the dishonesty comes in. And the inevitable consequences are always negative feelings.'

There was a long, long silence. Toad felt quite exhausted. At one level he was trying to understand these ideas intellectually. But at the deeper level of the unconscious, these ideas were touching his very self and stirring up an emotional confusion. He wanted to be on his own and to let these ideas wash over him and take him where they would. He did not know exactly where this would be, but he felt sure it would be in the direction of growth.

Heron saw that Toad was deep in introspection and so he said, 'I think it's time to finish now,' and so the session closed. But as Toad was on the point of leaving, he turned to Heron and said, 'I'm feeling a bit confused. I know that these ideas about games and life positions are very important but I need time to explore them further. I feel that you have only skirted around the area and I don't really understand it all.'

'You are quite right,' answered Heron. 'These ideas are both important and difficult and we have only just touched on them. Let us use our next session to examine them in greater detail, especially psychological games. Shall we do that?'

'Thank you,' Toad replied. 'That's just what I would like to do. See you next week.' And off he went.

14

Playing games or winner loses all

'What will help you most', said Heron, as he started their next session, 'is to realise the connection between the games people play and their life positions. You do remember life positions, don't you, Toad?'

'Very clearly,' said Toad and he went to the flip-chart that was hanging on the wall, rifled through the pages and opened it at Heron's diagram of the previous week.

'Good,' said Heron. 'In that diagram you can clearly see the four life positions, with one position represented in each of the quadrants. What I propose we do is look at each position in turn and try to understand the kind of games people are likely to play. What do you think of this approach?'

'Yes, that's fine by me,' answered Toad. 'Can I choose which life position we start with?'

'Of course,' said Heron. 'Which one will you choose?'

Toad turned to a fresh sheet of paper and wrote 'I'm not OK; you're OK'. Then he said to Heron, 'Now what does that really mean?'

'It means', said Heron, 'that it is the behavioural attitude of someone who thinks poorly of himself and feels other people are better than he is.'

'Better at what?'

'Better at almost anything,' replied Heron. 'People who have low self-esteem usually feel that not only has life dealt them a poor hand, but it has also dealt other people a better one. In general terms, people in this position feel that they are life's victims and so they play games which result in them being victimised.'

'Like what?' asked Toad.

'I'm So Unlucky,' replied Heron.

'Beg pardon?' said Toad, in some surprise.

'That's the name of the game. It's played by people who believe that they are unlucky and who will readily supply you with a long list of all the unlucky things that have happened to them. For instance, some people will blame their misfortune on the house they are living in, or even its geographical position on supposed leylines and just think of all the superstitions that concern bad luck, like breaking a mirror or spilling salt.'

'But we can be unlucky, can't we?' asked Toad. 'For instance, I've never won a raffle in my life and I don't suppose I ever shall.'

'I am talking about something much more serious,' answered Heron. 'I'm talking about people who go out of their way to select and remember the sad and unhappy events and forget and discount the good times.'

'That seems a very depressing way to lead your life,' said Toad.

'That's a very observant remark,' Heron responded, 'because people who play this game *do* get depressed. They feel that bad forces are affecting their lives which they can't control, and this makes them feel anxious and inadequate.'

'What about another game?' asked Toad, after a pause.

'PLOM,' answered Heron.

'Oh, I remember that one,' Toad said quickly. 'It means Poor Little Old Me and at one of our sessions you accused me of playing it!'

'Yes, I did mention it before, but I don't think I accused you of playing it,' Heron said. 'My aim is not to accuse you but to help you recognise the games you are playing so that you can give them up.'

'Do you really think I play this game?' Toad asked.

'Well, what do *you* think?' responded Heron. 'Certainly at the start of our sessions, you were suffering from an acute attack of self-pity, wouldn't you say?'

'Yes, you're quite right. I did feel that everyone was picking on me, especially when I first returned home after my adventures. I certainly felt very depressed and inadequate then. I've always wanted people to love me, no matter what I do.'

'Now that's another game,' said Heron.

'What is?'

'Love Me No Matter What I Do. Some people make messes or get into scrapes just to see how far they can go before someone stops forgiving them or rejects them. "There you are," they can say. "That proves that I really am that bad or that stupid."'

'These games seem very dangerous to me,' said Toad. 'Because if someone you love or respect gives up on you, you certainly would feel miserable and all on your own.'

'I agree,' said Heron. 'You are beginning to realise how dangerous these games can be – that they can seriously damage your health.' There was a pause as they both sat quietly in deep thought. After a while, Heron asked, 'Toad, what do you think is the most extreme behaviour that a person who feels "Not OK" can take?'

Toad said in a quiet voice, 'Suicide, I suppose?'

'Yes,' said Heron. 'Now of course, I'm not saying that

everyone who feels "Not OK" is going to kill himself. But did you know that suicide is one of the major causes of death in young men in England?'

'No, I didn't know that,' Toad replied, 'but I can believe it. I have been in that situation and it is very desolate. And frightening.' He sat quietly as he remembered how close he had once come to the abyss. After a while, Heron spoke.

'What Ego State do you think people are in when they play these victim games?'

'Sad Child, I should think,' replied Toad. Then with more vigour he said, 'No, I shall be more positive. It's definitely the Sad Child State. I can speak from experience. I know.' And again he was silent.

'Shall we look at another of the Life Positions?' asked Heron after a while, and he wrote 'I'm OK; you're not OK'. 'Do you understand what this position means, Toad?'

'I think so,' said Toad. 'It must describe someone who thinks that he or she is better than other people. So I suppose they will play games to reinforce this. Is that right?'

'Yes, it certainly is,' answered Heron. 'These are usually games where the player can be angry, or at least critical or judgemental. People in this psychological position often get into positions of power and authority and then they can play their game.' He wrote on the flip-sheet 'NIGYYSOB'.

'What on earth is that?' asked Toad.

'It is the initial letters of the name of the game. They stand for "Now I've Got You, You Son of a Bitch".'

'That's an ugly-sounding game,' said Toad, who could be quite fastidious about the proper use of English.

'Yes,' answered Heron. 'And it's an ugly game to play.'

'So what happens?' Toad asked.

'Well,' said Heron, 'this game is frequently played at work. First of all, someone makes a mistake which, as you can imagine, often happens. The boss then notices it, calls in the erring subordinate and proceeds to give him or her a dressing down, shouting and raving at them out of all proportion to the offence committed. As you can see, this game allows the angry person to get angry, apparently justifiably, thus confirming the "I'm OK; you're not OK" Life Position. They have the proof that other people are essentially incompetent and unreliable, and second, that it is their duty to chastise and punish them. "Otherwise", they say, "they will think they can get away with it!" '

'Phew,' exclaimed Toad. 'I can sympathise with anyone who has been on the receiving end of that game. It reminds me all too clearly of my father when I was little. And not so little. I can see now that NIGYYSOB was one of his favourite games.'

'Unfortunately, this game seems to be on the increase, especially in organisations,' replied the Heron. 'It's all too easy for people in authority to act out their phantasy of the punishing parent and treat their staff like naughty children. The papers seem to be full of cases of bullying. In your case of course, you had no one to whom you could appeal.

'There are other games played from the "I'm OK; you're not OK" position which you may recognise,' continued the Heron. 'Such as "Why Do You Always Let Me Down?"'

'Good heavens,' said Toad. 'That's Father again. He was always saying that.'

'Or playing it,' Heron interjected.

'Yes,' answered Toad. 'He played it regularly with me.

It always worked. I ended up feeling useless or guilty and he, I suppose, was confirmed in his belief that I was useless and that he was a superior being. Do you think that's right, Heron?'

'I'm afraid so,' Heron replied. 'It will have confirmed his feelings of moral superiority and it is often associated with another game, "How Dare You!" '

'It seems as if people in this Life Position always need to attack and condemn,' said Toad.

'You have got it exactly,' said Heron. 'These are the persecutors who use any opportunity to create situations where they can judge and punish others. It is interesting to wonder just what are their own internal persecutors that lead to this behaviour.' After a pause he asked, 'What do you think is the most extreme behaviour that a person who feels "I'm OK; you're not OK" can take?'

Toad paused for a moment and then said, 'Murder, I suppose.'

'Yes,' replied Heron. 'Fortunately, few people go that far. But you will hear people say about a boss at work, "It's murder working for him!" And they mean it.'

'So presumably people in this position play games from the Parent State?' mused Toad.

'And always from their Critical Parent,' added Heron. 'These people are quick to criticise, anxious to get angry and want to judge others by impossible standards. Of course, sometimes they may make a pretence of being in their Nurturing Parent, when they say things like, "This hurts me more than it hurts you" or, "I'm doing this for your own good", but most of us can recognise hypocrisy when we hear it. But there is another interesting thing about people in this psychological position,' continued Heron. 'They rarely, if ever, get depressed.'

'Why is that?' asked Toad in some surprise.

'Because anger is such a good defence against depressing thoughts,' answered Heron. 'Angry people never feel guilty, because they always blame others. They defend themselves by projecting their internal fears outwards on to others, so they can be angry with them instead of with themselves.' Toad looked puzzled, so Heron said, 'Let me give you an illustration of what I mean. Suppose that someone in the "I'm OK; you're not OK" position has ordered a taxi which fails to arrive. When this happens, how will he feel?'

'He will probably feel very angry,' Toad answered. 'I can imagine Badger getting in quite a rage and playing NIGYYSOB with the taxi firm over the phone.'

'Exactly,' said Heron. 'But now imagine a similar situation, only this time the person is in the "I'm not OK; you're OK" position. How will *he* feel?'

Toad considered this new situation and didn't like what he saw. 'He won't get angry,' he answered, 'that's for sure. But after that, I don't know what he would do.'

Heron then said, 'Imagine it is you, Toad, in that situation. There you are waiting for a taxi which hasn't arrived. How will you feel?'

Toad thought for a while and then said, 'I suppose I will start to feel sad and wonder why the driver has forgotten me. I might think that he has many other important calls and that I'm at the bottom of the list.' Then after a pause he said, 'I might even blame myself and think that maybe I hadn't made the arrangements properly.'

'So you can see the difference?'

'Yes, of course I can,' replied Toad with some vehemence. 'And what implication am I supposed to draw from that? That I should get angry like Badger and tell people what I think of them and shout and rave? Is that what you think I should do?' He paused and then he looked directly at Heron and said, 'I suppose you think that I am "Not OK" and that I am a complete wimp. Is that it?'

'No, not at all,' answered Heron. 'These ideas are not to be used as labels with which to attack or insult people. They are simply ways of trying to understand behaviour, especially our own.'

'You sound quite defensive,' said Toad. 'And I am not attacking you. But I have to say that, at this minute, I am feeling quite angry with you. I've felt it boiling up for some time and now I want to let it out.' Heron tried not to look surprised, but he was. 'You always seem to be getting me to admit my faults and failures,' Toad continued, 'and yet you never tell me directly what you think of me. All this time, you say "What do *you* think, Toad? How do *you* feel, Toad?" You never tell me what you think of me, and yet you're supposed to be the qualified counsellor, whatever that means. And sometimes you seem just like my father. Well, I think I've had enough!' He sat in his chair and confronted Heron directly.

There was complete silence. Finally, Heron said, 'So what are you going to do about it?'

Toad almost exploded. 'There you go again. More questions. Let me tell you, I've had just about enough of your bloody questions.' He looked at Heron, as if daring him to speak. He could feel his heart beating strongly, but it wasn't pounding. He realised that, although he was genuinely angry, he was in complete control of himself. He was also aware, without fully understanding it all, that he had just done something of great significance which somehow involved both Heron and his father.

If he were to be honest, a part of him felt frightened at what he had just done. He had not just been rude to

Heron. He had taken him on and in some way, over-thrown him, and somehow this had also involved his father. Suddenly he felt that he no longer needed to play the subservient role. He could assert himself and say what he wanted to say. Although he realised that he would have to deal with the new situation that this would inevitably cause. For instance, how would he deal with Heron now?

'I'm sorry about that,' he said eventually. 'But I am not apologising. I have been wanting to say that to you for some time, and that seemed to be the right time. Do you understand?'

'I think so,' answered Heron. 'Do you want absolution?'

'No I don't,' said Toad. 'I stand by what I said. But I suppose that's the end of our counselling?'

'I think it is,' said Heron. 'But on reflection, I would like us to have one more session.'

'Why is that?' asked Toad. 'I really feel that our work is finished now.'

'Finished, yes, but not completed,' Heron replied. 'There are two reasons why I think we should meet for a final session. The first is that I would like you to have the opportunity to review what you have learnt here and what you intend to do about it. In other words, what changes you intend to make.'

'Yes, I can agree to that,' said Toad. 'And the second reason?'

'The second reason is that I think we should work together in this new relationship which seems to be forming between us now and try to understand what has happened.'

'I agree,' said Toad. Then he added, 'Thank you, Heron,' and they shook hands in a serious sort of way.

15

The final session

When Toad returned to the Hall, the first thing he did was to look at his diary. For a long time now this had been practically empty, except for his regular appointments with Heron. But recently his social life had begun to improve and there was an increasing number of entries.

When he had been in his depressed state and for some time before Mole had found him, Toad had experienced the most horrible ennui. Time seemed to stretch before him like a desert with no goals or signposts and each day brought only emptiness, robbing his life of purpose. He had forced himself to put some structure into his existence by going for a daily walk, and the counselling sessions had provided at least something to do between one formless week and the next.

Gradually, things had started to change as he began to feel better. It was as if the development in his inner world was reflected in his growing social life. For instance, in the previous week he had attended the AGM of the Bankside Cricket Club, where he was re-elected President unopposed. Everyone came and greeted him and said how pleased they were to see him looking so much better.

To his surprise and pleasure, he was presented with a new club tie, in the tasteful colours of lime green, mauve and chocolate. He was cheered as he removed his bow-tie there and then and replaced it with the new one, and all of this gave him very warm feelings. He also realised that, with the coming season, Saturdays would be taken up with cricket, and he entered these in the diary. His desert of loneliness was starting to bloom again.

Looking through his diary, Toad also saw with pleasurable anticipation another entry, which was for lunch at the Red Lion Hotel in a few weeks' time. He had only yesterday received this invitation from the Rat, to what was described as a 'Celebration Lunch'. Because he wasn't sure what was being celebrated, he had telephoned Rat and asked him. To Toad's great surprise, Rat had answered, 'Your recovery, of course, and we shall all be there!'

But perhaps the diary entries which gave the strongest evidence of Toad's changed attitude were those which referred to 'My New Venture'. Previously, work and Toad had always seemed incompatible, due mainly to his early fears of having to work for his father in the brewery. But as he reflected on his work with Heron, Toad realised that his continued development and improvement required purpose, and purpose required work. For too long, his wealth had cushioned him from the need for employment and his inner strength and resources had become soft and flabby, like an athlete who had stopped training. But now he was feeling altogether different. What he wanted to do now was to compete – and to win!

Carefully and gradually Toad was making plans for his future. This had resulted in meetings with two of his past acquaintances, both of whom were now working in the City. He had also held meetings with the family bankers and for the first time looked closely at the accounts and understood the parlous state of Toad Hall and its estates. All this spurred him on to think about what he really wanted to do, and gradually an idea began forming in his mind: he wanted to start his own business!

He was not at all worried when, to his surprise, Heron telephoned to postpone their next meeting. He apologised and suggested another date in three weeks' time. This in fact had suited Toad well, as he had already arranged some more meetings concerning his new venture and needed the extra time. Finally they agreed to meet on the morning of Toad's lunch with his friends, and as he entered this new appointment in his diary, he ringed both events to indicate their importance to him.

When that day dawned, Toad woke early and lay awake in bed, thinking about what might happen at his final session with Heron. He was a little apprehensive about the meeting and, if he only knew, so was Heron. When they had last met three weeks ago, it had resulted in a curious situation which neither of them fully understood. Toad knew he had got angry with Heron and yet he knew that he had not lost his temper. Heron knew that Toad had fought him in some significant way and yet he had not been rebellious. Somehow, this event had been productive and full of meaning and had changed their relationship. But neither was sure what would happen next.

After breakfast, and seeing that it was a lovely morning, Toad decided to cycle, and he was soon spinning along the lanes that took him to the Heronry. Propping his machine against the wall, he rang the bell for the last time and waited for Heron to open the door. They greeted each other formally and sat down in their usual places.

'Well, Toad,' said Heron, 'so this is to be our last meeting.'

'Yes it is,' answered Toad. 'It will seem strange not to come here again.'

'Do you know how many meetings we have had?' Heron asked.

'As a matter of fact, I do,' Toad said. 'I was going through my diary. Discounting that first and rather disastrous meeting, we have had ten sessions. It seems like more.'

'Does it?' asked Heron. 'It certainly seems a long time ago since you first came here and I asked you how you were feeling. Do you remember what you said then?'

'I remember very well,' replied Toad. 'I cried and rated myself one or two on your feelings scale.'

'Well, you are certainly looking brighter now,' said Heron. 'At that first meeting, you looked very sad and despondent. But now you are looking alert and happy.' Toad was certainly looking well. There was more colour to his cheeks and his large eyes were clear and bright. He was wearing a check suit which he had recently bought and this was complemented by his new cricket-club tie.

'So how are you feeling now?' Heron asked.

'I was wondering when you would get around to asking me that,' said Toad smiling. 'I am certainly feeling much better in myself. My appetite has returned and I am sleeping normally. You know, at one time I was sleeping very badly and waking up so early. Why was that?'

'It's hard to say precisely but it is one of the recognised symptoms of people who feel depressed,' Heron said. 'I expect it was connected with your inner fears. When you are feeling like that, anxious thoughts come into your conscious mind and prevent you from relaxing. It is as if they sound alarm bells inside you to tell you that all is not well – in the hope that you might do something about it.'

Toad thought about that for some time and then said, 'You are probably right. But I also have a lot more energy now. Not just physical, but mental. At one time I couldn't seem to get interested in anything, it all seemed too much effort. You know, I could hardly read the newspaper. But that's all different now. I've started to make plans for the future. I don't mean just good intentions, like New Year's resolutions, but real plans involving details and dates for action.'

'Good,' said Heron, 'so how is all this making you feel right now?'

'Well, I know that this might sound banal,' Toad replied, 'but I am feeling happy. I actually look forward to each day as full of exciting, new possibilities, whereas not so long ago, everything seemed so pointless. That's a real change, isn't it?'

'It certainly is,' Heron replied. 'So where are you now on the Feelings Thermometer?'

Toad replied immediately. 'Today I would put myself at nine. It could almost be ten, but I want to reserve that for later, in case things improve even more.'

'So how do you feel about other people?' asked Heron.

'It's funny you should ask me that,' Toad answered. 'I don't know why, but when we first met, I had lost interest in my friends and what they were doing. In fact, they almost seemed to have become my persecutors. But I certainly don't feel like that any longer. Now I'm really interested in what they are all doing and', he added, 'I hope they are interested in me.' He told Heron about the lunch he would attend after this session and what he intended to reveal.

'So, no more suicidal thoughts?' asked Heron matter-of-factly.

'No, none at all,' Toad replied. 'I feel that I can now take life much more as it comes. But I shan't forget how low I felt. The memory of it will always be there, perhaps as a kind of reminder of what life is like at the boundaries.' He sat looking solemn.

After a little while, Heron asked, 'So how would you describe yourself now?' Toad got up and went to the flip-chart and opened it at the page which showed the Life Positions.

'Could I be in the "I'm OK; you're OK position"?' he asked. 'It feels almost like tempting fate, but that's how I feel.'

'That's bravely chosen,' said Heron.

'Why do you say "brave"?' asked Toad. 'That is really how I feel.'

'It's brave', replied Heron, 'because in selecting that position you not only make a choice, you also make a commitment. For life.'

'What exactly do you mean?' asked Toad, looking puzzled.

'I mean that being in the "I'm OK; you're OK" position is a dynamic, not a static state. You can't get there and say, "That's it. I've arrived", as if you have just conquered Everest. Being OK, and believing that others are, requires behaviour and attitudes which continuously demonstrate this, both to yourself and others. And it is certainly not a shelter from the slings and arrows of outrageous fortune.'

'I see,' said Toad. 'You mean that to say "I'm OK; you're OK" is really an act of faith?'

'Yes, I do,' answered Heron. 'It is very near to being the Humanist's credo, a belief in oneself and others which does not require a belief in a god or the supernatural.'

'You make it sound very solemn,' said Toad.

'If by "solemn" you mean full of importance,' Heron replied, 'then I don't disagree.'

There was silence, then Toad said, 'Our relationship has changed, don't you think, Heron? There was a time not so long ago when, if you had said that to me, I would have felt that you were putting me down because I had said something stupid. But now I can think about it and see if I agree with you or not. That's certainly a change, isn't it?'

'It is,' said Heron. 'And do you think that this change in our relationship has come about because of me or because of you?'

'I know what the right answer to that is,' said Toad with a smile. 'I'm sure that you want me to say that it is due to the changes in me. And, to a great extent, I agree. I know that I have changed. I don't feel so dependent on you and I can challenge you without feeling that I'll get a reprimand.' He paused and then added, 'But I have to say that I think you have changed as well.'

'In what way?' asked Heron.

'You don't seem so dogmatic or critical. At one time I used to look to you for the slightest sign of your approval or disapproval. Although I have to admit that you usually looked impassive and hid your feelings.'

After a pause, Heron said, 'So from what you have just been saying, how would you describe our relationship during the sessions?'

'I don't know if you meant it to be so,' answered Toad, 'but a lot of the time I felt that it was a parent–child relationship. I frequently felt dependent on you and I was always hoping that you would give me some wise words which would provide the answer.'

'And did I?' asked Heron.

'No, not really,' Toad replied. 'You have certainly taught me a lot and this has been very helpful, but you never gave me answers. What I now realise is that you were always trying to get me to answer my own questions, getting me into the Adult.' He paused and then added, 'But now, quite recently, we appear to have a much more relaxed relationship. Especially since last session. That seems to have been a milestone in my development.'

'It's interesting that you should say that,' Heron replied, 'because I was thinking that during our work together you have gone through what I can only describe as the process of growing up psychologically.'

'In what way?' asked Toad.

'I mean', answered Heron, 'that when you first came here you were in a state of dependency, like a child, just as you have described. You were expecting to receive answers and you were constantly looking to me for signs of parental approval. Of course, I tried not to do this and I kept throwing the ball back to you by asking, "What do you think?" and "How do you feel?" And that made you angry.'

'It certainly did!' Toad answered with some feeling. 'I used to feel so annoyed with you. And you know how my anger finally boiled over and what happened at our last meeting.'

'I do,' said Heron. 'And I can see now that it was a very important step in your development. You behaved like a teenager standing up to his parent. You faced up to me as the pendulum of your feelings had swung from dependency to feeling angry and a wanting to reject me. In fact, you were being counter-dependent.'

'I was?' asked Toad. 'So why should that event seem so significant to me now?'

'Because', answered Heron, 'you transferred feelings which you had towards your father on to me. In dealing with me, you at last dealt with him. You actually found the strength and courage to act like a man and not like a child. In doing that, you grew up and moved into adulthood and as you asserted your own authority, you acted independently.'

'I see,' said Toad after a while. 'So you think that in our work together, I have moved from being dependent to feeling counter-dependent and then finally to being independent. Is that right?'

'Yes I think it is,' Heron replied. 'In counselling, we work not only with our brains but with our feelings. Whilst you can begin to understand behaviour intellectually, you can only fully understand yourself through getting in touch with your own emotions. As these become clearer to you, you realise that your feelings are not optional extras that can be ignored, but they are the very centre of your self.'

'I see,' said Toad again thoughtfully. 'So when I got angry with you last time, are you saying that I changed as a result of that, because my feelings were genuinely engaged?'

'Yes I am,' said Heron. 'You did emotional work and you learnt directly through the event. Whenever our emotions are genuinely engaged, there is the opportunity for growth. This is true experiential learning, which is how we have learnt anything of importance, right from birth.'

'That sounds rather anti-intellectual, learning through our emotions,' said Toad. 'What about all our schools and universities? Aren't they all dedicated to helping people learn through their intellect rather than through their emotions? Don't we need to be able to solve problems and keep our emotions out of things?'

'That's perfectly true,' Heron replied. 'People know how to do this and work hard to improve their technical excellence. At this moment, for instance, more and more managers are dealing with bigger and bigger technical problems than ever before. There are more people in education than at any previous time. Our colleges and business schools are chock-a-block. The world of intelligence and IQ is thriving. We have never before known so much about our physical world. . . .' Here Heron paused and then asked quietly, 'But what about the world of EQ, emotional intelligence? Just how much do we know about that?'

'I remember you mentioned this once before,' said Toad, 'but I didn't understand it then. What does EQ really mean?'

'It means', said Heron, 'understanding your own inner emotional life and being able to control it. And you can see that this is totally different from IQ.'

'So what's someone like who has a high EQ?' asked Toad.

'In a nutshell,' replied Heron, 'they have great self-awareness and know their own emotions. They can manage their own feelings and bounce back from sadness and misfortune. But perhaps most importantly, they can control their impulsiveness and delay gratification, so avoiding hasty and ill-considered decisions and actions.'

'Hm,' said Toad, 'I'm learning up to the last minute. So far I have never been very good at delaying gratification. And that got me into all sorts of trouble. But I hope I have become a little more emotionally intelligent since working with you.' He paused and then said, 'Is there any more about EQ?'

'Yes there is,' replied Heron. 'It concerns understanding other people. Someone with a high EQ can recognise how someone else is feeling. You know that this skill is called "empathy". But perhaps the greatest skill that results from emotional intelligence is the ability to form good relationships with others, through understanding and handling their emotions. And that leads me on to make my final point before we finish.' Toad was sitting stock-still and paying the greatest attention to all that Heron was saying.

'Emotional intelligence allows you to go further in the direction of your own growth and development because with it you can move on from being independent to being interdependent.'

'What does that mean exactly?' asked Toad.

'Independency', replied Heron, 'implies a sort of pride in being yourself, with all your unique talents and differences, and a readiness to defend this new-found autonomy, like a nation gaining its freedom from a colonial past. And there is nothing wrong with that. But being interdependent suggests a maturity and self-acceptance, together with an acceptance of others in spite of their differences. Being interdependent allows you to relate effectively with others and cooperate with them, both socially and at work.'

'Yes, I can see that but— '

Toad was never to finish his sentence for the Heron suddenly interrupted him. 'Toad, just look at the time! We are fifteen minutes late. I'm so sorry. I've been going on rather, I'm afraid. I do apologise because I know you have another engagement immediately after this.'

'That's alright,' said Toad. 'I've really enjoyed this session and it won't matter if I'm a bit late for lunch.' They both got up from their seats and walked down the hallway, where Toad collected his overcoat from the hallstand and put it on.

'Oh, Heron,' he said, 'I almost forgot.' And he reached into his pocket and took out a package wrapped in brown paper. 'This is for you. It's a small "thank you" present.'

'That's very kind of you,' said Heron. 'Shall I open it now?'

'Yes, go ahead,' answered Toad. 'It's only a little thing.' Heron opened the package to reveal a small, beautifully turned wooden bowl, with the light and dark grains highly polished.

'I made it myself from a walnut tree which blew down at the Hall,' Toad continued. 'I've always liked wood-turning and I thought you might like this as a little reminder of our work together.'

'Thank you very much,' said Heron. 'I shall always treasure this. It will remind me of all the things I have learnt from our work together.'

'Really?' asked Toad in some surprise, 'I didn't know that *you* were supposed to learn anything. I thought it was only me.'

'Well, you're quite wrong there,' Heron replied. 'In counselling, learning is always a two-way process, although we each learn different things. But off you go now Toad, else you will be late for your lunch. Goodbye.'

'Goodbye Heron,' said Toad. 'And thank you.' And he got on his bicycle and rode off in the direction of the Red Lion, never to see Heron again.

16

Farewells and new beginnings

It was Rat who decided that Toad's recovery should be marked by a lunch. 'It's too easy', he said, 'to let significant events pass by without notice or celebration. Perhaps this is because we usually only recognise their importance after the event.'

For reasons best known to himself, Rat chose to hold this event in the Red Lion, an old coaching inn with a central courtyard and wood-panelled dining-rooms. The waiters seemed as old as the building, with drooping moustaches and long, white aprons which reached down to their cracked black shoes.

Even before Rat entered, he knew what the menu would be: Brown Windsor soup, roast Norfolk turkey with chipolatas, followed by sherry trifle, some dry cheddar, coffee extra. He arrived first in order to check that the private room he had booked was properly laid up. Rather to his surprise, the appearance of the room (called the Isis Room) was excellent, the table laid with a gleaming white starched cloth and napkins, sparkling glasses and heavy, old-fashioned cutlery.

He studied the wine list and, as he expected, saw several wines of good vintage and reasonably priced. He ordered a couple of bottles of claret and then repaired to the bar to await the arrival of the others. He ordered a pint of his favourite beer, 'OBJ', which stood, appropriately, for 'Oh Be Joyful!' and, in a spirit of great contentment, leaned on the bar and quaffed his ale.

The next to arrive was Toad. He was feeling relaxed and at ease and was looking forward to meeting his friends and telling them all that had happened. But as he walked casually through the courtyard, having leant his bicycle against the hotel railings and straightened his new cricket-club tie, his legs turned to water. For he recognised exactly where he was and the events associated with the place flooded over him. For this was *the* Red Lion, the very inn where, having escaped from his reforming friends years ago, he had eaten an enormous lunch and then (oh horror! he could scarcely continue) he had stolen a beautiful motorcar and driven straight to prison.

Luckily, at that moment Rat appeared at the hotel doorway and in his sensitive way he said, 'Hello Toady, you look as if you've just seen a ghost. You're the first to arrive. Come on in and I'll buy you a drink.' Regaining his composure somewhat, Toad followed Rat into the bar. The oldest waiter gave him a long and enquiring look, but Toad was able to stare back and handed him his coat to hang up.

'What'll you have then?' asked Rat. 'A pint of bitter?'

'Certainly not,' replied Toad. 'You know I always have a brandy and soda.'

'Nonsense, Toad,' replied Rat with some spirit, 'I can remember many times when you've had a beer.'

'Name one,' said Toad, practising his new-found assertiveness.

Fortunately, before the discussion could become too heated, Mole and Badger arrived together. They had shared a cab and Badger, as usual, had managed to get Mole to pay.

'Hello, Badger. Hello, Mole.'

Soon they were all standing in a group at the bar and talking animatedly.

'Good idea of yours, this lunch, Ratty,' said the Badger in his kindly way. 'Well done.' Rat half thought he might have his head patted. Toad was telling Mole one of his tall stories and Mole was saying 'Really' and 'Then what happened?', but in fact he had heard it before and was thinking about lunch.

At that point, the old waiter came in and said to Rat, 'Lunch is ready now, sir, if you would like to go in.' So in they trooped and were soon eating their soup and tucking into their turkey, helped down with liberal glasses of the excellent claret which Rat had chosen. Then there was the sherry trifle, which actually had some sherry in it.

'That's unusual,' said Badger. 'Usually the chef merely waves the cork over it.'

Toad and Mole both had seconds and then cheese and coffee were served, by which time everyone was feeling mellow and contented. Toad was about to take out a very large cigar from his cigar-case, when a stern look from Badger made him replace the offending weed, patting his pocket as if he were merely looking for his handkerchief.

'Well,' said Badger, smiling affably at all of them, 'so what are you all planning to do now?' There was silence. Small animals do not usually do much forward planning. Regularity and rhythm, within the framework of the changing seasons, provide the comfort that keeps anxious thoughts at bay. To change involves risk, and risk could bring danger, and danger means threats.

But after all they had been through and learnt about themselves, change had already happened to them and they knew they had to move on, whatever the risk. They were all growing up and learning how to put away childish things. So it was inevitable that each of them had made plans, even though, so far, they had not shared them with each other.

'Shall I start then?' asked the ever-helpful Mole. There was a chorus of agreement, and so Mole continued, 'I'm going back to Mole End. I'm going to turn it into a restaurant.'

The Rat, who had no knowledge of this, blurted out, 'But you can't cook for toffee. You can't even boil an egg!'

'Go and boil your head,' said Mole under his breath, but in a louder voice, 'I shan't be doing the cooking. I've got a very good chef. Do you remember Otter's young cub, Portly, who once got lost but we found him? Well, he's quite grown up now and seems to have been touched by the gods. He can cook the most delicious fish dishes, and his desserts are a delight. His speciality is bread and butter pudding. We are going to open it soon and it will be called "The Garibaldi".'

'I remember now,' said the Rat. 'I only visited your house once, but it was a very snug and compact place, and you had a bust of Garibaldi in your garden.'

Mole smiled with pleasure. 'You remembered, Ratty. I'm so pleased. And do you remember the rest of the garden – the goldfish pond with the cockle-shell border and the silvered glass ball that reflects everything all wrong? Well, that is where the restaurant will be. Otter is putting up the money and will be my partner. But I shall manage it and Portly will be the chef.'

'Well done, Mole,' said Badger. 'I shall come and

patronise you frequently. I like my grub, I do.' Badger could be remarkably vulgar when he chose.

'I'll be there too,' said Toad. 'What a ripping idea. When will you open?'

'Probably in the autumn,' replied Mole. 'You know, when most animals are fairly quiet and beginning to slow down and will appreciate the particular ambience of Mole End.'

'I know exactly what you mean,' said Badger, who welcomed the undergroundness of Mole's house.

Mole continued, 'And then, in the spring, we shall do picnic-hampers. You know, coldtonguecoldhamcoldbeef-pickledgherkinssaladfrenchrollscresssandwichespotted-meatgingerbeerlemonadesodawater, that sort of thing.'

I wonder where he got that idea from? thought Rat, remembering their very first picnic together on the river, but said nothing.

Mole stopped. He realised that, until recently, he would have been much more shy and reticent in speaking. Now he was the centre of attention and was describing his plans clearly and interestingly. He felt stronger and happier than he had done for a long time.

He leaned over to the Rat and said quietly, 'You will come, won't you, Ratty?'

'Of course, Moley. I shall be your most regular customer.' Ratty smiled his twinkly smile and they both knew they would stay firm friends, in spite of Mole returning home.

'Well, how about you then, Ratty?' Toad asked. 'What will *you* do now that you will be all on your own?'

Rat swallowed hard. He had known for some time that this would be an awkward moment, but it had to be faced. Looking into the middle distance, rather than directly at any of his friends, he said, 'I am leaving the river bank!'

'You're going to do what?' asked the Badger in his severest tones.

'I am going to leave the river bank. In fact, I am going to move to a grey, seaside town in the South. It's a lovely little place with a harbour which has one steep side with tall stone houses and gardens running down to the rocks.' Rat's voice had become stronger and his eyes glistened as he visualised the place he was describing. 'When you look down the flights of stone steps, overhung with great pink tufts of valerian, you see patches of sparkling blue water. The harbour is full of little boats tethered to the rings and stanchions of the old sea wall. And all the time a small ferry boat keeps chugging from one side of the harbour to the other, taking people to work and bringing them home again.

'When you walk out of the town, there is a pretty beach where you can shrimp and where they serve cream teas on trays and you can eat sitting on the rocks. In the spring, all the woods and pathways that wend their way along the cliff-top are carpeted with primroses and violets, and you can climb up and look out to see ships from all over the world sailing in and out of the harbour, their sails billowing white like the clouds above them.' Ratty stopped. His friends knew that he liked to write poetry, but this was the first time they had heard him speak like this. They were entranced.

'But', Toad said gently, 'won't you be lonely without us?'

'No, not exactly,' answered the Rat. 'You see, I shall be renewing the acquaintance of an old friend of mine. He was a seafaring rat from Istanbul. I hadn't seen him for ages, but recently he wrote to me from that seaside town in the South, offering me a job. He owns a small book-shop called "Wayfarers All" which specialises in travel and he wants me to manage it. Apparently it's just opposite the parish church and it only takes a minute to walk down to the town quay. I shall live above the shop and although it will be very different from my beloved river bank, I mean to make a go of it.'

'Well, Ratty,' said the Mole, 'you have surprised me, you really have. But as you were talking, I remembered how, long ago, you became obsessed with "going south", as you called it and I almost had to fight you to make you see sense. Are you sure this isn't just another attack of southern fever?'

Rat smiled. 'No Mole, this is quite different. It is true that those memories have lingered and, in fact, that was when I first met Alessandro, my sea-going friend. But since then I have carefully considered what I want to do and what differences this change will make to my life. You will always be a close friend, Mole, but I must move on. And besides,' said the Rat quietly, 'I am going to write a book.'

'About what?' asked Toad.

'Perhaps about you, Toady. And you, Badger, and you, Moley and about all the adventures we have had. For no matter what happens, those memories are so vivid that I can run them like a film through my head.'

'What will you call it?' asked Mole.

'I'm not too sure at the moment. Perhaps "The Breeze in the Bushes".'

'Not much of a title, that', said Badger disparagingly. 'You need something more gripping to gain the public's attention. How about "Boats and Badgers"? That sounds much more exciting.'

'We shall see,' said Rat. 'As I said, I am still undecided,

but if I can write the book, I know I can find the title.' He had known it would be difficult to break the news of his departure to his friends and when he had started to speak he had felt extremely anxious. But once he got going, he knew what he wanted to say and he knew he had said it well. In fact, he had practised in front of the bedroom mirror until he felt confident, even deciding when to speak softer and when to pause for dramatic effect. And he had been effective. But not too effective, thought Rat. I don't want them down all the time visiting me for a holiday.

The waiter brought more coffee and a dish of petit fours and everyone helped himself. Toad and Mole began to quiz Rat about his plans, which left Badger sitting rather impatiently and looking pointedly at his pocket watch.

'So I expect you all are wondering what *I'm* going to do?' he asked.

'Yes of course we are,' said Toad warmly. 'You know we are. It's just that Mole's and Rat's plans are so surprising and exciting.'

'And you don't think mine will be, is that it?' Badger asked aggressively.

'No, of course it's not that,' said Rat. 'Tell us your plans.' And stop acting like a baby, thought Mole, at the same time looking at Badger with polite interest.

'Well, all right,' said Badger, somewhat mollified. 'But you all need to pay attention, like Mole here, because I have some very important news.' The others composed themselves, feeling that they had just had a 'wigging' from the headmaster.

'As you all know, for a number of years I have given a great deal of my time to local affairs and I have been proud to represent the many simple and mainly honest folk who live in the Wild Wood. There are many important issues which have to be dealt with, like keeping out the developers who want to build horrid bungalows on the edge of the wood and which would increasingly encroach on where we live. Or stopping them building a road through a part of the wood, for your wretched poop-poops, Toad.'

Toad was about to protest and say that that was a long time ago and nowadays he bicycled everywhere, but Badger's stern looks and loud voice made him keep quiet and look suitably apologetic. But as Badger went on, Toad knew that what he was saying was true. Badger was a patrician and, not surprisingly, many of the smaller animals in the Wild Wood looked to him for a lead in local issues and felt safe under his protection.

Badger had got elected on to the Parish Council and then on to the Wild Wood Rural District Council and had worked hard to protect the wood and its inhabitants. In another age he would have been a 'green', but for Badger it just seemed natural to preserve the habitat where they all lived and on which they depended for their sustenance and life itself.

'My philosophy has always been', Badger continued, his half-moon glasses on the end of his nose giving him an air of wisdom and authority, 'that there should be One Nation and, therefore, One Wood. We need to integrate people, not split them apart and drive them into factions. Those of us who have been blessed with this world's goods have a responsibility towards the deserving poor and I like to think that I have contributed towards this by setting up our local Woodlands Hospital, of which I have the great honour to be Chairman.' He paused, waiting for the round of applause, but none came.

Well I'm blowed, thought Mole. He's a blessed Tory and it's as if he's giving us his election manifesto. I'm not having that. Does he think I'm one of his deserving poor? I'll show him! But Badger moved on, allowing no room for interruptions.

'Individual freedom, with a proper concern for the less fortunate, can only exist within the framework of the law. Those who break the law must be punished, and punished severely if the crime warrants it.'

At these words, Toad had gone pale and was fingering his tie as if it were preventing his breathing. The memories of his appearance in court before the magistrate and his subsequent incarceration could still come back and give him the horrors.

'I say, Badger,' said Rat, 'steady on! Remember who's here.'

Badger stopped instantly. Although he could be pompous and bossy, he could also be warm and caring. 'I say, Toad. I didn't mean you. I just wasn't thinking. Careless of me. Please forgive me.'

'All right,' said Toad, 'but I am still very sensitive about that issue.'

'Of course you are,' replied Badger. 'I have always believed that if someone pays their debt to society, as you have, Toad, then they should be fully rehabilitated and integrated into society.' At these kind and generous words, Toad felt much better and poured himself another coffee.

'So when I was appointed Chairman of the local bench', Badger continued, 'it seemed to me that my different activities combined to form a lifetime, if I may say so, of service to my fellow creatures.'

Mole knew that Badger was proud of his achievements and not at all reticent about his activities and appointments. In fact, the brass plate by Badger's dark green door, just below the iron bell-pull which Mole so clearly remembered from one of his most terrifying adventures, had recently been replaced. The new plate, neatly engraved in square capital letters, now read 'MR BADGER, JP'.

'Well,' said Toad, who by this time was growing slightly impatient, 'you mean that you are going to carry on doing the same things you are doing now.' Badger gave him a very stern look. 'Not that there's anything wrong with that,' Toad added hastily. 'Life of service, commitment to the community, that sort of thing. Very important.'

Mole started to giggle, but a sharp kick from Rat on an old wound on his shin made him stop.

'If you would only listen, Toad, you would hear the really important news that I am going to impart.' They all waited expectantly and Badger, looking extremely important, said, 'I have been asked to stand as the Parliamentary Candidate at the next election!' For a moment, everyone was silent. Then they found their voices and came up to Badger and shook his paw and clapped him on the back and congratulated him and Badger enjoyed every minute of it.

'I can just imagine you as our MP,' said Rat. 'You could always make a good speech, you are as straight as a die and you have a genuine concern for everyone on the river bank and in the Wild Wood.'

In spite of his differing political views, Mole knew a good animal when he saw one and, before he knew it, he was shouting, 'Three cheers for Badger. Hip-hip hooray. Hip-hip hooray. Hip-hip HOORAY!'

Badger was genuinely moved by this spontaneous show of affection and regard and wiped his eyes on the red cotton handkerchief he always carried. There was much talking as everyone told everyone else what a good MP Badger would make and how they were not at all surprised by the news and Badger was saying how he would welcome help with addressing envelopes and that sort of thing. Gradually the talking trailed off into silence and Toad found that his three friends were looking at him with an air of expectation.

'Well, come on Toad,' said Mole. 'We're all waiting to hear *your* plans. I'm sure they will be absolutely wonderful.'

Poor Toad! He had been rather dreading this moment, for it reminded him of another time when he had had the opportunity to amaze his friends with his scintillating wit and song, and then had thought better of it. That was some years ago now, at the banquet he had given to celebrate the reoccupation of Toad Hall. Then, as now, he would have liked to take the stage and amaze and delight his friends with his great oratory, or perhaps a stirring song sung in his pleasing tenor voice.

But he knew now that this would be inappropriate and not express what he really wanted to say. Toad the Great Entertainer, Master of a Thousand Disguises, Terror of the Roads, was a fantasy and a dangerous one at that. Whenever he had adopted one of these roles, it always ended in tears, or worse. At that previous banquet he had behaved in a modest and unselfish manner only because he feared the wrath and displeasure of Badger, whom he had seen as a severe and critical parent.

Now he chose consciously not to play the fool and remembered from his Sunday-school days the story of Polycarp. A venerable and scarcely remembered saint, Polycarp was about to be martyred when he heard a voice saying, 'Be strong, Polycarp, and play the man!' So Toad said to himself, 'Be strong now and play the Toad!'

'Well, look, you fellows,' he said quietly yet firmly, 'I certainly have made some plans which will have a great effect on my life. Although you may think them dull. You see, I've taken a job.'

'What?' said Badger in utter amazement, 'you mean you are going to undertake paid and gainful employment?'

'Yes I am,' replied Toad, looking Badger unflinchingly in the eye. 'In fact, I have already started.' Rat fidgeted in his chair. Trust old Toady to amaze us, he thought.

'But what is it?' Rat asked. 'What exactly are you going to do?'

'I am going into estate management. As you all know, I have spent a lot of my time managing the Hall. It's not been all caravanning and driving fast cars, you know.' Here Toad tried to look severely at Mole, but he could not keep it up. He started to grin and then he laughed with Mole and then all the others joined in. (That's nice, he thought. For the first time that I can remember, they are laughing *with* me, not *at* me.)

'No, but seriously, you chaps, there is a lot of work to do on the estate, seeing the Hall Farm is properly managed, cutting and planting timber, that sort of thing. So I've got together with a couple of others and, using the money which Father left me, we are going to set up our own estate and property business. Because of my particular experience, I shall be looking after the better end of the market, such as Riverside Residences and Country Estates (the snob end more like, thought Mole).

'I have to tell you, Toad,' said Badger, 'that I am both pleased and delighted. I know that your father would be equally pleased and not a little surprised. Well done, Toad.' These words were music to Toad's ear.

'What will your company be called?' asked the practical Rat.

'We shall be called "Knight, Toad and Frankly", and we are setting up our offices in London. We are currently negotiating for premises in the Strand.'

'Did you say London?' asked Mole in rather an anxious voice. 'Isn't that in the Wide World, to which I thought we never went or even referred?'

'Tosh!' said Toad spiritedly. 'There's a great deal of nonsense talked about the Wide World. Of course, when you are small and have only lived in a restricted community, it can appear big and threatening. But after a bit you can find your own place in it and play a much bigger role. I believe I can gain more autonomy there and there are certainly more opportunities to be had.'

(Well, he may be right, thought Mole, but I'm glad I'm not moving. I know the river bank and it knows me. And if that's a restricted community, then I'm all for it.)

'So will you be staying at the Hall?' asked Rat.

'No. I've sold it.'

There was a stunned silence at this news. Badger was horrified. 'You've done what? You've sold Toad Hall? You know what they will do with it, don't you? They will turn it into an hotel or, God forbid, a safari park with foreign animals which have no right to be here.'

'Calm yourself, Badger,' said Toad, controlling the situation most ably. 'I have sold it to a group of business-men who are going to turn it into a Management College. We have agreed that the main building will stay untouched. . . .'

'It has to,' interrupted Badger. 'It's a listed building.'

'Although no doubt they will need to build a bedroom block and other facilities,' continued Toad, quite calmly. 'To tell you the truth, it's a burden off my shoulders. The Hall was getting increasingly expensive to maintain. The

West Wing needs re-roofing and the kitchen needs to be completely refurbished.'

'So where will you live?' asked Mole.

'I have bought a house in the village, the Old Rectory. I'm sure you know it. It's quite a nice late Victorian house, with a manageable garden and lovely views across the valley. And it means that I can easily walk to the station and catch my train to the City.'

'Presumably travelling first class and not on the foot-plate,' said Rat rather pointedly.

Toad was about to be quite angry but instead he laughed and said, 'Yes, Ratty, I shall be travelling quite legitimately and not pretending I'm a washer-woman.'

'Toad,' said Mole, 'you never cease to amaze me! Since the first time I met you, many years ago, I have always found you exciting and larger than life. I know you have got into all sorts of scrapes but at least you have lived an exciting life. Compared to me, I feel you have drunk life's experience to the last drop. So won't you find your new life rather dull, just being "something in the City"?'

'Mole, you really are the most perceptive creature! You have spoken the thoughts that at one time I dared hardly admit to my consciousness. There certainly has been a lot of excitement in my life: stealing cars, escaping from prison, being a master of disguise, outwitting the police. Oh yes, I've had some excitement, that's for sure.' Here Toad's voice was starting to rise and he began to puff himself up. But he quickly realised what was happening and resumed a calmer disposition. He coughed and then continued, 'I have decided to join the local Amateur Operatic Society. That way I can have fun playing a role on stage, rather than getting it mixed up in real life. And without conceit and after a thorough audition, I have been given the lead in their next production.'

'Well done, Toady. Good old Toady,' his friends chorused, showing their genuine pleasure. 'What's the part?'

'I am to be the Pirate Toad. I wear a hat with the skull and crossbones on it, a striped jersey and an eye-patch.'

'Sing us one of the numbers, oh please do,' asked Mole, imploringly.

'Yes, come on Toad,' said Badger. 'This is one of my favourite comic operas.'

'Very well,' said Toad, 'but you must join in the chorus.' He waited for silence and then he started. His voice was clear and melodious and he was able to strike just the right note of mock-heroics. After each verse the others joined in the chorus, which consisted of these words:

Toad	For I am the Pirate Toad
All	Hurrah for the Pirate Toad
Toad and all	And it is, it is a wonderful thing
	To be a pirate Toad.

By this time, all the friends were laughing and singing, and Toad was getting into the spirit of things and was in danger of singing the whole of the first act, when there was a knock on the door. The old waiter came in and said apologetically, 'I am sorry, gentlemen, but have you finished? We have to clear away and prepare the room for another event this evening.' Rat looked at his watch and was amazed to see that it was almost six o'clock. Coats were fetched, goodbyes said, and everyone went out into the cool, clear evening.

The taxi, which had been waiting for some considerable time in the yard, drove up to the front entrance and Mole and Badger got in. The driver was about to give them a piece of his mind for being kept waiting but, when he saw that it was Badger, he decided otherwise and wished him a good evening. They drove off, with Mole waving out of the window. Rat sauntered off down the road, swinging his cane, thinking about summer at the seaside and imagining what kind of a boat he might buy to sail in the harbour when he moved south.

Toad put on his bicycle clips, pulled out a flat cap from his overcoat pocket, adjusted it to the correct angle, mounted his machine and pedalled off towards the Hall. His head was full of what he was going to do, and he was feeling in a very good frame of mind. He recalled how his friends had reacted to the news that he was starting his own business and especially what Badger had said to him. He's not such a bad old stick, he thought, I think I dealt with him rather well. And he found himself humming a tune he had not thought of for ages. As he remembered it more clearly, he began to sing the words softly to himself with great enjoyment.

'The world has held great heroes,
　　As history books have showed.
But never a name to go down to fame,
　　Compared to that of Toad!'

He laughed with delight when had sung this. 'Well,' he said, 'it's only a bit of fun. And actually, it's not a bad poem.' And so he decided to sing the remaining verses. Only this time, because there was no one about, he sang them at the top of his voice, only finishing as he cycled up the drive of Toad Hall, breathless but happy.

'The clever men at Oxford
　　Know all that there is to be knowed.
But they none of them know one half as much
　　As intelligent Mr Toad!

The animals sat in the Ark and cried,
  Their tears in torrents flowed.
Who was it said, "There's land ahead"?
  Encouraging Mr Toad!

The army all saluted
  As they marched along the road.
Was it the King? Or Kitchener?
  No. It was Mr Toad!

The Queen and her Ladies-in-waiting
  Sat at the window and sewed.
She cried, "Look! Who's that *handsome* man?"
  They answered, "Mr Toad".'